St. Petersburg

A Portrait of a Great City

By Vincent Giroud

The Beinecke Rare Book & Manuscript Library

Yale University

Distributed by

University Press of New England

This book accompanies the exhibition
St. Petersburg: A Portrait of a Great City
at the Beinecke Rare Book & Manuscript Library
Yale University, New Haven, Connecticut
October 23, 2003–January 17, 2004

Cover illustrations are details
from Four Panoramic Views of St. Petersburg
by John Augustus Atkinson,
London [c.1802]
Yale Center For British Art, Paul Mellon Fund

Library of Congress Cataloging-in-Publication Data
Giroud, Vincent.
St. Petersburg : a portrait of a great city / by Vincent Giroud.
    p. cm.
"This catalog accompanies the exhibition 'St. Petersburg: A Portrait of
a Great City' at the Beinecke Rare Book & Manuscript Library,
Yale University, New Haven, Connecticut, October 23, 2003–
January 17, 2004."
ISBN 0-8457-3153-X
1. Saint Petersburg (Russia)—History—Exhibitions. 2. Saint
Petersburg (Russia)—In art—Exhibitions. 3. Beinecke Rare Book
and Manuscript Library—Exhibitions. 4. Manuscripts—
Connecticut—New Haven—Exhibitions. I. Beinecke Rare Book
and Manuscript Library. II.
Title.

DK542.G57 2003
016.947'21—dc22   2003019897

ISBN 0-8457-3153-X

PRINTED IN THE UNITED STATES OF AMERICA

In memory of Laura K. Lada-Mocarski

Contents

Introduction

Few cities of old Europe—save perhaps for Paris and Venice—have inspired a fascination comparable to the one exerted by St. Petersburg since its founding three hundred years ago. Created literally ex nihilo by Peter the Great in May 1703, decreed capital of the Russian empire a mere ten years later, it was widely admired as one of Europe's handsomest towns half a century after its founding, thanks to the embellishments it received under Empress Elizabeth. By Catherine the Great's death in 1796, it had become a cultural capital as well as a political one. Described by countless—if not always uncritical—visitors throughout the nineteenth century, its development is intimately linked to the incomparable flowering of Russian literature and the arts from Pushkin to Tolstoy, from Glinka to Tchaikovsky, from Briullov to Repin. The early twentieth-century avant-garde had one of its finest hours there, with Diaghilev, Bakst, Bely, Akhmatova, and Mandelshtam among its most illustrious representatives. Stripped of its original name after 1914, when it became Petrograd, then Leningrad as of 1924, deprived of its status as capital in 1918, martyred by a long siege during the Second World War, it appeared to be on its way to becoming a locus for remembrance and nostalgia. Yet, miraculously, it has managed to preserve or rebuild its architectural glory, while its intellectual and cultural prestige have survived and revived. The restoration of its original name by popular referendum in 1991, the jubilee celebrations in the spring of 2003 can be, and have been interpreted as the signs of a renaissance of the "immense and proud" city of Pushkin's poem.

This tercentennial exhibition was not a vain attempt to present in New Haven a comprehensive account of St. Petersburg and its history. Its more modest purpose was to offer a portrait of this great city with a selection of some highlights from the Yale collections. The first part of the display is devoted to the history of Petersburg during its first century. The second part focuses on accounts of the city by Western European travellers and visitors, from Kotzebue to Verdi. The third illustrates Petersburg's third century with a few, inevitably limited images, centering on one of Yale's most famous treasures, the Romanov family albums, exhibited for the first time in their entirety in more than two decades, and ending with the emblematic figure of Anna Akhmatova.

The exhibition was part of a series of events held in the fall of 2003 to celebrate the city's founding. The initiative of this commemoration is to be credited to Alexander M. Schenker, professor emeritus in the Yale Department of Slavic Languages and Literatures, whose own splendid contribution to the tercentennial celebrations, *The Bronze Horseman*, which retraces the history of Falconet's monument of Peter the Great, coincided with the publication of this catalogue. No words could adequately express our gratitude to Professor Schenker, not only for the inspiration he provided throughout this project, which owes much to many conversations and exchanges with him over the years, but also for the generous loan of two items from his personal collection. I am particularly indebted to him for letting me read proofs of his book and for the suggestions and corrections he contributed to this catalogue. All remaining errors are mine.

The project of a St. Petersburg exhibition and related events received from the outset the enthusiastic support of the director of the Beinecke Library, Barbara A. Shailor, now Deputy Provost for the Arts at Yale. My gratitude goes to her and to the members of the organizing committee she convened, and from whose advice I greatly benefited. I wish to thank in particular Professors Vladimir Alexandrov in the Slavic Department and Paul Bushkovich in the History Department, Suzanne Boorsch, curator of prints, drawings, and photographs at the Yale University Art Gallery, and Tatjana Lorkovic, curator of Slavic and East European Collections at the Sterling Memorial Library. Last but not least, I wish to thank Una Belau, coordinator of the whole commemorative event, for her help and advice, especially during our preparatory trip with Barbara Shailor, in September 2002.

One of the highlights of the exhibition is without doubt the splendid copy of Sadovnikov's panorama of Nevsky Prospect from the collection of Paul Mellon. For this loan, for the loan of two books preserved in the Yale Center for British Art, and for permission to use the Mellon copy of the Atkinson views featured on the cover of this catalogue, we are deeply grateful to Amy Meyers, its director, and to Elisabeth Fairman, curator of rare books and archives, and her colleagues, whose help has been invaluable. I have also benefited from useful comments from Scott Wilcox, curator of prints and drawings at the Center, and I am happy to thank him as well.

We are equally grateful to Sterling Memorial Library and the Yale Arts Library for the loan of the Tsarskoe Selo copy of Rusca's *Disegni* housed in the Arts of the Book Collection, whose curator, Jae Rossman, has been most helpful in making it available to us.

I should not forget to convey my thanks to several colleagues in the Beinecke Library who have been of particular help, notably Stephen Parks, curator of the James Marshall and Marie-Louise Osborn Collection, who kindly brought to my attention the three manuscripts from that collection included in the display, and to Christa Sammons, who, in addition to editing this catalogue (and thereby saving me from much embarrassment), contributed one book from the Yale Collection of German Literature. Timothy Young, assistant curator of modern books and manuscripts, provided much needed, diligent assistance, especially in coordinating the scanning of the illustrations under the expert care of Matthew Shirley and his team, to whom I also wish to express my gratitude. James Mooney expertly helped with its editing and Greer Allen, as always, deserves heartfelt thanks for his design as well as for his unfailing good humor and patience.

Hubert Nyssen kindly provided the identification of the film mentioned in Nina Berberova's memoir and gave permission to quote from it. I am much indebted to Marie-Hélène Girard and to Stephen De Angelis for guidance and advice and, as so often, to Ellen Cohn and her colleagues in the Franklin Collection for their gracious and competent assistance. It is a special pleasure to acknowledge one among the many antiquarian bookdealers who have enriched the Yale collections in this particular area: as soon as he heard about this forthcoming celebration, Rodolphe Chamonal in Paris has been a splendid source of rare, unusual, and unique items relating to St. Petersburg, some from his own collection. Without him, this exhibition and catalogue would have been much poorer.

Yale has had the singular privilege of being blessed during its long history—which coincides within two years with that of the city we are celebrating—with the extraordinary generosity of donors collecting in particular fields. Valerian and Laura K. Lada-Mocarski were such donors in the area of Russian history and travel, and, especially, accounts of Russia by Western travellers, from Herberstein to Custine and beyond. Polly Lada-Mocarski endowed a fund which continues to foster acquisitions in this domain, while providing assistance to research. One wish that was particularly dear to her was that items from the collection formed by her and her husband should be regularly displayed for the enjoyment and instruction of all, beyond the confines of the Beinecke reading room. This exhibition, which has attempted to fulfill this wish, is dedicated to her memory.

Finally, I wish to express my gratitude for the gracious and friendly benevolence extended to me, during the few years of our acquaintance, by Prince Alexander Romanoff and his wife Princess Mimi. It had been my hope that Prince Alexander would honor the opening of this exhibition with his presence. His death in the late summer of 2002 was cause for great sadness. To his memory as well this catalogue is dedicated.

Andrei Ivanovich Bogdanov. *Istoricheskoe, geograficheskoe i topograficheskoe opisanie Sanktpeterburga, ot nachala zavedeniia ego, s 1703 po 1751 god . . . so mnogimi izobrazheniiami per'vykh zdanii; a nynie dopolnennoe i izdannoe, nadvornym sovietnikom, praviashchim dolzhnost' direktora nad novorossiiskimi uchilishchami, Vol'nago rossiiskago sobraniia, pri Imperatorskom moskovskom universitetie i Sanktpeterburgskago vol'nago ekonomicheskago obshchestva chlenom Vasil'em Rubanom.* Sanktpeterburg, 1779.

This first detailed record of the urban development of St. Petersburg was prepared in 1751–52 under the authority of Empress Elizabeth, Peter the Great's daughter, who reigned from 1741 until 1762. The author, A.I. Bogdanov (1692–1766), was a librarian at the Academy of Sciences. His work remained unpublished until 1779, when it was issued in an augmented edition by Vasilii Grigor'evich Ruban (1742–95), a court officer, with a dedication to Catherine the Great and 84 plates, maps, and plans by Nikita Chelnakov, Nikolai Kirtsanov, and A.G. Rudakov.

Chelnakov's woodcut frontispiece portrait of Peter, "Emperor and autocrat of all Russias," can be seen as an allegory of the founding of St. Petersburg. The emperor is depicted as both a military and a political ruler: over his uniform, he wears a ceremonial robe; he holds the scepter, while the crown is placed on a pedestal behind him. His right foot rests on a cannon, symbolizing his victory over the Swedes of Charles XII; the pair of drums on the ground seems to imply that the country is now at peace. The books piled at Peter's left foot appear to represent his own passion for learning and his determination to open Russia to arts and sciences — as well as his passion for book collecting on a vast scale. Next to the books is the plan of the Peter and Paul Fortress, which is also seen standing in the background, with the spire and towers of the Peter and Paul Cathedral. It is nearly dwarfed by two large ships in the offing, symbolizing both the importance of St. Petersburg as a port and Peter's wish to open the country towards Western Europe.

This highly symbolic image freezes in an instant the first two decades of the history of the city, which began with the establishment of the fortress on 16/27 May 1703 on a small island in the Neva. On 29 June the feast day of St. Peter and St. Paul, the site was officially given the name of St. Petersburg. Built chiefly of wood, the fortress was completed in September of the same year. At the same time, Peter had a small house erected for himself outside the fortress, while the Admiralty, market, and embryonic port and trade infrastructure were also started. The future of St. Petersburg, however, was not firmly established until Peter's definitive victory over the Swedes at Poltava in July 1709 and the conquest of Livonia the following year. In 1717, the year when the town was officially declared capital of Russia, the first real urban project was proposed by the French architect Jean-Baptiste Alexandre Le Blond, who worked in St. Petersburg from 1716 until his death three years later. The number of households in the city had by then grown to 4,500. The somewhat crude illustrations in Bogdanov's book show numerous examples of the houses built during the first fifty years of Petersburg's history as well as its early churches, palaces, and monuments, thus preserving images of many buildings that have not survived.

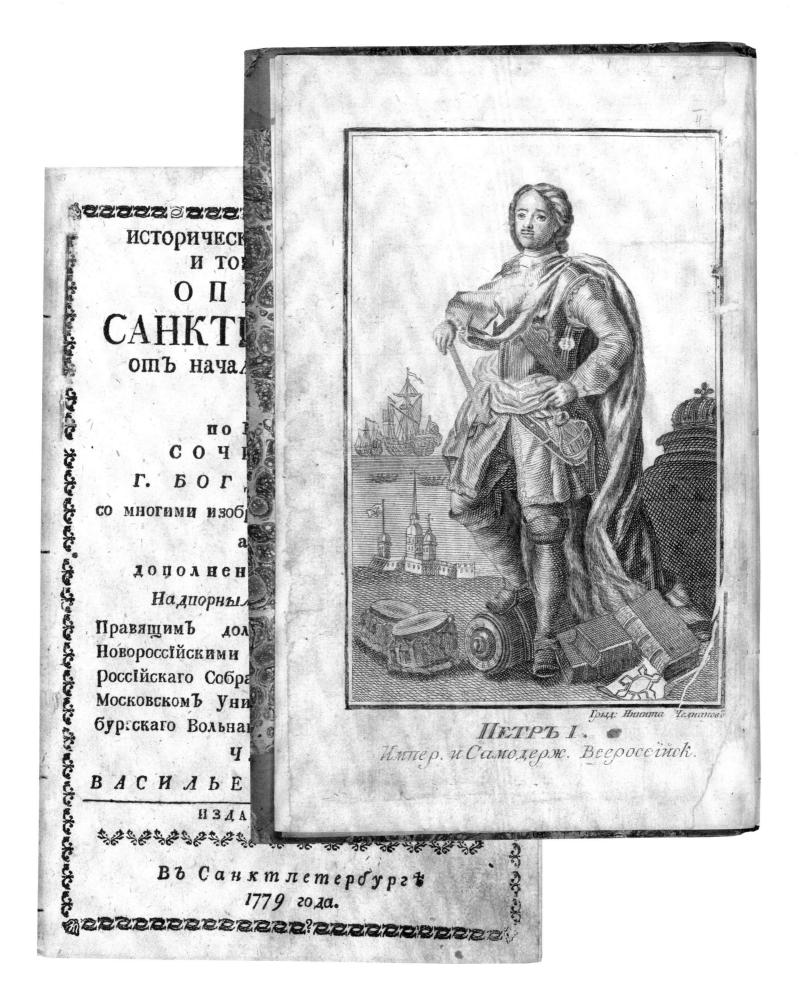

ИСТОРИЧЕСК...
И ТО...
ОП...
САНКТ...
отъ начал...

по...
СОЧ...
Г. БОГ...
со многими изоб...
а...
дополнен...
Надпорныл...
Правящимъ дол...
Новороссійскими...
Россійскаго Собра...
Московскомъ Уни...
бургскаго Вольна...
Ч...
ВАСИЛЬЕ...

ИЗДА...

Въ Санктпетербургѣ
1779 года.

Грыд: Никита Челнаковъ

ПЕТРЪ I.
Импер. и Самодерж. Всероссійск.

John Deane. Manuscript account of Peter the Great, 1724.

The author of this 60-page manuscript, John Deane (1679–1761), was an English sea captain who served in the Russian navy from 1712 to 1722. He later served for 17 years as British Consul at Ostend, later retiring near his native city of Nottingham. His account of Peter the Great, whom he had several opportunities to approach in person, was compiled following his return from Russia. It begins with the general observation that "the Czar is universally regarded as the Wonder of the Age; and, in many Cases, to do him Justice, is, incontestably, a Great Man, as well as a Great Prince." Then follows a lively vignette of a day in the life of Peter in the city to which he gave his name:

"A Judicious Eye, taking a Critical Survey of the Immense Toile, for 30 Years past, sustain'd by this Indefatigable Prince, will be struck with Admiration at his Great Qualities: especially, observing him, in such a Variety of Imployments, in his New City of St Petersburgh, in 60 Degrees of North Latitude, where, consequently, Daies very Short in Winter, frequently, several Hours before Daylight, in the College of War, Admiralty, Senate, Privy Court of Inquisition, or Cabinet, giving Directions in Affairs of the highest Importance; afterwards, hurrying to the Yards, consulting with his Shipbuilders, improving the Theory, or advancing the Practic, by Working hard with the Ax, or Adze; scarce allowing himself time to eat; and, after Dinner, in an Apartment of the Palace, accommodated with a Master, and proper Utensils, amusing himself in turning Tobacco Stoppers, Snuff Boxes, &ca; and, the same Evening, at an Assembly, in the House of some Grandee, conversing familiarly, all Ceremony excluded, with people of all Ranks, from a Prime Minister to a Captain in his Navy: None of inferior Condition being admitted, unless of Noble Families. Persons may be in these hither Parts of Russia, converse with Foreigners, and see the Czar often; and, yet, not perceive any thing Contradictory to his Amiable Character: and thus forming Superficial Notions, pronounce 'em as Oracles to Mankind; whilst still this Prince's Real Temper remains, in a very great Measure, Unknown."

If the above account conforms with the "official" image of the hyperactive founder of Petersburg, Deane's portrait of Peter the Great is, in fact, by no means adulatory. While, as a sailor, he cannot fail to commend the tsar's interest in, and knowledge of maritime matters, he dwells on his cruelty (with due reference to the trial and death of Tsarevich Alexis) and evokes, in highly colorful terms, the corruption and licentiousness of his entourage—"Menchecoff" (Aleksandr Danilovich Menshikov) being singled out in opprobrium. If he does not specifically discuss the planning of St. Petersburg, Deane nevertheless makes revealing comments on the difficulties of the entreprise as he saw it, less than 20 years after the city's founding:

"The Czar has said, were he to build St Petersburgh again, this City shou'd be seated in Vasilley Oustra, the Island Prince Menchecoff obtain'd; and the Whole shou'd be form'd into a Regular Fortification, to secure his Darling Place from the Incursions of Parties in Case of Adverse Fortune in War: and, since Menchecoff has been declining in his Master's Favour, Others are directed to build there; but, few are able, and fewer willing; so the Work goes on but Slowly. The Russians look upon this City as the Ruine of their Nation; and, indeed, the Nobility, and Gentry, that have no Employments, and, consequently, no Opportunity of Squeezing their Fellow Subjects, are reduc'd to the lowest Ebb; being compell'd to build their Houses, and live in a place, where it stands them in more by the Month, than wou'd handsomly maintain them a Year in the Country: Many, beginning to build, are unable to finish; Others have the Shell of a House, but not wherewith to provide Furniture; ¾ of their Annual Income of their Estates being taken from them for Taxes, or One Pretence, or Another. and yet, besides this St Petersburgh, 4 Magnificent palaces are carrying on . . ." As it turned out, the plan to develop the city on Vasilievsky Island, as had been advocated by Le Blond, was as short-lived as it was impracticable, and the island, save for Menshikov's palace and several administrative buildings, remained largely unoccupied for another century or so.

Deane is otherwise remembered for the wreck of his ship the *Nottingham* in 1710, off the coast of Maine, an event subsequently reported by Cotton Mather in his 1711 pamphlet *Compassions called for*. William Henry Kingston's 1870 "boys' book," *John Deane of Nottingham: his adventures and exploits*, concerns itself with Deane's life prior to his Russian stay, which it mentions only in passing. Nor does it refer to the gruesome circumstances of his death, following an attack by robbers in a field near his house.

The Czar is universally regarded as the Wonder of the Age; and, in many Cases, to do him Justice, is, incontestably, a Great Man, as well as a Great Prince. The Astonishing Progress made, in cultivating the Minds, and polishing the Manners, of the Barbarous Russ; in forming, out of a rude Multitude, a very Great, and well disciplin'd, Army; and establishing, from Comparatively Nothing of that Kind, a Royal Navie of Ships of War, as well built as Any in the World, besides a great Number of Gallies, and other Vessels, of almost every Individual Sort in Use; evinces, beyond Controversy, an Imperial Genius.

History affords very few Instances of Russian Embassies, in the Time of the Czar's Predecessors; but, of late, not Lewis, the 14th, ever used more peremptory Termes, than are to be seen in the Russian Memorials, given in to Most of the Courts in Europe: whilst the Purport of Those, to China in 1714, and 1719; and to Persia in 1715, evidence his Vast Designs. And, even, a Judicious Eye, taking a Critical Survey of the Immense Toile, for 30 Years past, sustain'd by this Indefatigable Prince, will be struck with Admiration at his Great Qualities: especially, observing him, in such a Variety of Imployments, in his New City of St Petersburgh, in 60 Degrees of North Latitude, where, consequently, Daies very Short in Winter, frequently, several Hours before Daylight, in the College of War, Admiralty, Senate, Privy Court of Inquisition, or Cabinet, giving Directions in Affairs of the highest Importance; afterwards, hurrying to the Yards, consulting with his Shipbuilders, improving the Theory, or advancing the Practice, by Working hard with the Ax, or Adze; scarce allowing himself time to eat; and, after Dinner, in an Apartment of the Palace, accommodated with a Master, and proper Utensils, amusing himself in turning Tobacco Stoppers, Snuff Boxes, &c.; and, the same Evening, at an Assembly, in the House of some Grandee, conversing familiarly, all Ceremony excluded, with People of all Ranks, from a Prime Minister to a Captain in his Navy: None of inferior Condition being admitted, unless of Noble Families. Persons may be in these hither Parts of Russia, converse with Foreigners, and see the Czar often; and, yet, not perceive any thing Contradictory to this Amiable Character: and thus forming Superficial Notions, pronounce 'em as Oracles to Mankind; whilst still this Prince's Real Temper remains, in a very great Measure, Unknown. For, many things must necessarily concurr, to qualifie a Man to draw a Just, and Exact, Portraiture of his Personal, and Political, Disposition: One of his own Subjects dares not; and a Foreigner, of some Capacity, must spend some Time to learn the Russian Language, and Exotic Customs; and have an Imployment, at least, Occasionally, near his Person, authorizing an immediate Application to him for Orders and Instructions, on sudden, and different, Emergencies; when the Soul appears undisguis'd in it's Genuine Sentiments; and, after this, becoming Independent of the Court, have an Opportunity of making Observations, in the remote Part of his Dominions, of the Inclination of the Populace;

Friedrich Christian Weber. *Nouveaux mémoires sur l'état présent de la Grande Russie ou Moscovie. Où l'on traite du gouvernement civil & ecclésiastique de ce pays; des troupes de terre & de celles de mer du Czar; de ses finances, & de la manière dont il les a réglées; des divers moyens qu'il a employé pour civiliser ses peuples, & aggrandir ses Etats; de ses Traités avec différens Princes d'Orient; & de tout ce qui s'est passé de plus remarquable dans sa Cour; surtout par rapport au feu Prince Czarien, depuis l'année 1714 jusqu'en 1720. Par un Allemand résident en cette Cour. Avec la Description de Petersbourg & de Cronstot. Le Journal du Voyage de Laurent Lange à la Chine. La Description des moeurs et usages des Ostiackes. Et le Manifeste du Procès Criminel du Czarewitz Alexis Petrowitz. Avec une Carte générale des Etats du Czar, suivant les dernières observations.* Amsterdam: Mortir, 1725.

Weber was in Russia as Hanoverian minister from January 1714 to August 1719. His memoir, widely read across Europe, first appeared in Frankfurt in 1721 and was soon translated into English and French. The first part is a chronological account, containing many references to the development of St. Petersburg and life in the city (as well as a report on the trial and death of Tsarevich Alexis). Among other comments, Weber gives the figure of 40,000 workers employed in building operations in 1714. He also comments on the Russian nobility's reluctance to move to the new capital, despite their inability to resist the tsar's orders.

The book is supplemented with an 88-page "Description of Petersburg," a city Weber calls a "wonder of the world"; elsewhere he quotes Menshikov as describing it as "another Venice." Yet he remarks that the city is so spread out that "it looks more like a gathering of several villages than a city."

The description follows the engraved map which, in this edition, opens the second volume. Entitled "Plan of the city of Petersburg as it stood in 1716," it is in fact far from being an accurate document of the development of the town at the time, but rather a projection into a future that did not happen. This utopia reflects Peter the Great's desire at the time to expand the city on Vasilievsky Island. According to Weber's account, Peter became attracted to the site, which had not particularly caught his attention before, and "he resolved to build there, in regular fashion, the real city of Petersburg." The scheme was the work of Le Blond and the Swiss architect Domenico Trezzini (ca. 1670–1734), the first important architect in the history of St. Petersburg. It shows a perfectly geometrical grid, evoking a military encampment as much as a city, including two market squares and a rectangular public garden, as well as a system of canals that would have made the city look like Peter's beloved Amsterdam. "Admittedly," Weber adds, "most of the island is still woody or full of thick bushes, and that now only a small part of the land has been cleared; yet this would not be enough to prevent the execution of the tsar's design, since at the first command he gives, there are always several thousand people altogether ready to obey." In this particular instance, Weber was too optimistic in his prediction, since Vasilievsky Island, as we have already noted, was not fully developed until the middle of the nineteenth century.

A much more accurate picture of the city's actual development appears on the Admiralty side, where one can see the first traces of Nevsky Prospect, begun in 1712, which linked the Admiralty with the Alexander Nevsky Monastery. The following year, the French geographer Nicolas de Fer drew a map showing an even more geometrical plan of the city, incorporating Le Blond's and Trezzini's design for Vasilievsky Island and showing a large planned development on the eastern side of the Admiralty Island.

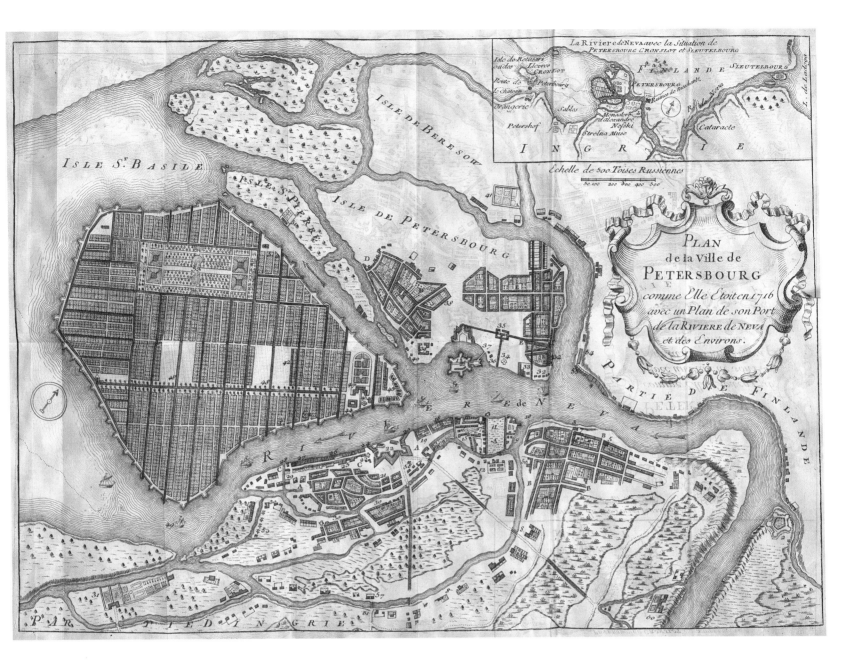

Johann Christian Trömer. *Des Deusch-Françoß Jean Chretien Toucement Adieu von alle Raritées was ßu St. Peterburg in Abondance ßu seh. An ihre Russ. keyßerlich Majestée très soumis presentir den 6. Decembr. 1735. en Compagnie ßu les. Ehn Gratulation an ganß alle Russland bey celebrir die grosse Memoir Tag von Entrée ßu Regierung Ihr Russ Keyßelich Majestée Anna Joannowna; ehn etwas an ihro hoch kräflich Excellence Err General Feld Marchal Kraf von Münich, wie sie verreiss von St. Peterburg; ehn Description von Peterhof. Ehn Neu Jahr Gratulation an Mons. Pedrill premier Durak ßu St. Peterburg. Ehn Suplique an Aeolus. Mit Explications von die fremde Wort.* Leipzig: Troemer, 1736.

The author of this poetic extravaganza in praise of Empress Anne is one of the most curious exponents of the late German literary baroque as it flourished at the court of Dresden. If not the inventor of the genre, Trömer (1698–1756) certainly amplified and perfected the peculiar fashion of writing in "Deusch-Françoß," i.e. German as if it were being pronounced like French. The opening of this "Adieu to St. Petersburg," following a visit Jean-Chrétien Toucement (as he called himself) paid to the city in 1735, captures the flavor of the piece:

Adjeu kross Peterbourg! die Du mackst so viel Bruit
in diese kansse Welt, ick wünsch Dir bonne Nuit
Dein Raritées ick ahb nu alle admirer,
darum ick will jeszund nack mein Land retournir;
wenn ick werd seyn kekomm in meine Papa Land,
dein kross Magnificence ick will mack all bekannt.

The opening poem is a sort of diary account of Trömer's stay in the form of an elaborate compliment to "Ihr Russich Majestée" (rhyming with "Admiraltee"), with respectful references to her German favorite, Ernst Johann Biron (alias Büren), Duke of Courland (1690–1772). A second poem, preceded by a decorative vignette including the words "Adieu mon cher Petersburg," is a series of farewells to various personages Trömer had commerce with in the Russian capital ("Adieu Err President von die Academie!") and to other features of the city ("Adieu du Neva Fluss mit Wasser und mit Eis!"). Thirdly, a "Gratulation" to Anne opens with the words "Triomphe et victoire" and ends with a special praise to Count Burkhard von Munnich (1683–1767), the Danish military engineer who built the Ladoga canal and was then in charge of the army. The last poem is a farewell to Peterhof, the imperial residence built by Peter the Great between 1714 and 1723.

Empress Anne (Anna Ivanovna or Ioannovna in Russian) was the daughter of Ivan V, half-brother of Peter the Great, and the widow of Friedrich Wilhelm, Duke of Courland. Her accession to the Russian throne in 1732, following a period of dynastic crisis, marked a return to favor of St. Petersburg, which Peter II had abandoned for Moscow. Anne transferred the court and government back to St. Petersburg soon after her coronation. The frontispiece to Trömer's book shows one of the festivities her reign became famous for, an illumination of the Peter and Paul Fortress, while spectators are watching, either from the shore or from the frozen Neva, some on foot, others on horseback or in sledges.

Die Festung St. Petersburg illuminirt an einem hohen Festin oder
Praſsdnik.

Georg Wolfgang Krafft. *Description et représentation exacte de la maison de glace construite à St. Petersbourg au mois de janvier 1740, et de tous les meubles qui s'y trouvoient; avec quelques remarques sur le froid en général, et particulièrement sur celui qu'on a senti cette même année dans toute l'Europe: composée et publiée en faveur des amateurs de l'histoire naturelle . . . Traduit de l'allemand par Pierre Louis Le Roy, membre de l'académie impériale de St. Petersbourg et professeur d'histoire.* St. Petersburg: de l'imprimerie de l'Académie des sciences, 1741.

The famous "Ice Palace" has remained a symbol of the baroque extravagance of the court of Empress Anne. It was erected on the Neva in January 1740 to celebrate the wedding of one of her ladies in waiting, of particularly unprepossessing physique, and Prince Mikhail Golitsyn, a convert to Roman Catholicism, who, as a punishment, was appointed court buffoon. The wedding was attended by representatives of all parts of the empire wearing their national dress.

The architect of the Ice Palace, Piotr Eropkin (ca. 1698–1740), was among the young Russian architects sent by Peter the Great to study in Italy. He also translated Palladio's *Treatise* into Russian. He played a leading role in the Commission of St. Petersburg buildings, which was created in 1737 to oversee city planning. He may have been the author of the new plan issued by the commission: this plan firmly established the future development of St. Petersburg on the Admiralty side along the "trident" formed by the three "prospects" (Nevsky, Gorokhovskii, and Voznesenskii) converging towards the Admiralty. This design, favored by Peter the Great himself, may have been inspired by Versailles, or by a similar arrangement from the Piazza del Popolo in Rome. In 1740, Eropkin was implicated in the plot to overthrow Anne's unpopular favorite Biron. Arrested along with the minister Artemii Petrovich Volynskii, his brother-in-law, Eropkin was accused of high treason and executed.

Presumably for this reason Eropkin's name does not appear in this account by the German scientist G.W. Krafft (1701–54), a member of the Imperial Academy of Sciences, who simply credits the empress and her chamberlain, Aleksei Danilovich Tatishchev. Krafft not only supplies a detailed description of the edifice, illustrated with plates showing its outside and inside, but also looks at it from a scientific perspective, both as a physicist and as a meteorologist (the winter of 1740 was one of the most rigorous on record).

Built on a spot facing the Admiralty following an unsuccessful earlier attempt across from the Winter Palace, the house comprised a vestibule and two rooms. It was surrounded by an elegant balustrade and guarded by ice cannons (which could fire real balls) and statues of dolphins which, at night, emitted burning naphta. On one side stood a lifesize statue of an elephant ridden by a Persian, while an ice steam bath house was built on the other side.

The house was decorated with columns and statues, and some of the architectural decorations were painted in green to imitate marble. "The building," Krafft writes, "which seemed to be of one piece, unquestionably made an infinitely finer effect than if it had been built with the rarest marble, its transparency and blueish color making it seem of much more precious stone than marble."

One could access the house through two entrances, leading into the vestibule, with four windows. The two rooms, with five windows each, contained ice furniture and utensils as well as working fireplaces.

Having fulfilled its ceremonial function, the ephemeral palace was opened to the public and drew many visitors until, in March 1740, it began to melt. Krafft notes that its remnants joined the ice reserves of the Winter Palace.

This architectural wonder inspired the 1833 novel *The Ice Palace* by Ivan Ivanovich Lazhechnikov, the "Russian Walter Scott." Alexandre Dumas discovered the book while he was in Russia, adapted it in French, and published it in serial form in his journal *Le Monte-Cristo* in 1858 at the same time as his St. Petersburg travel chronicles.

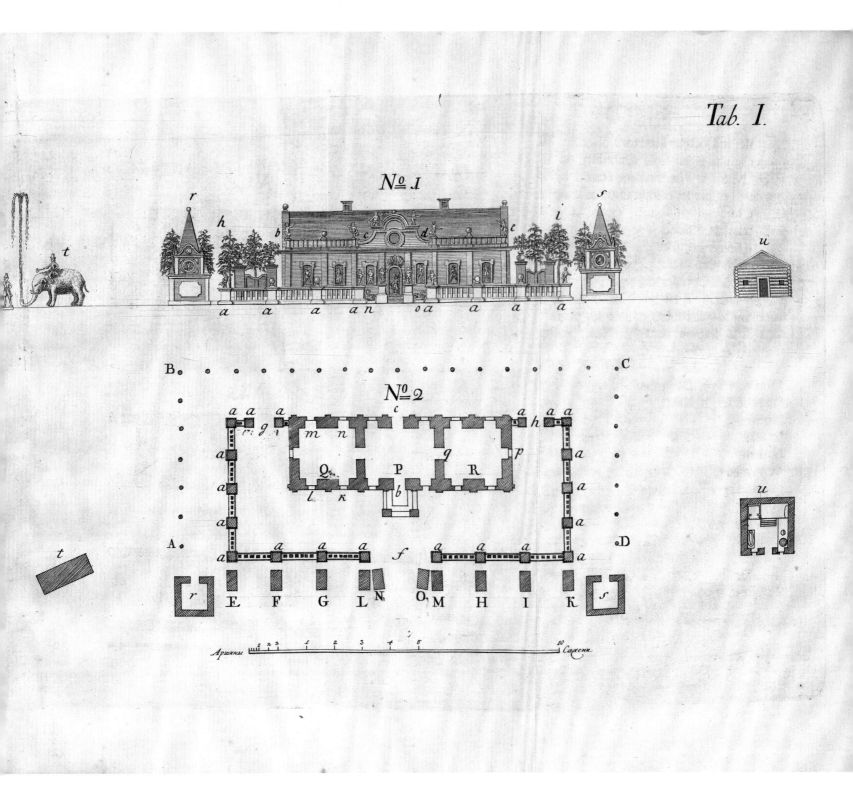

Tab. I.

N⁰ 1

N⁰ 2

Mikhail Ivanovich Makhaev. *Prospekt Gosudarstvennykh Kollegii s chastiiu Gostinogo dvora s Vostochnuiu storonu / Vüe des batimens des Colleges Imperiaux d'une partie du magazin de marchandises vers l'orient. Engraved by E.G. Vnukov. From *Plan stolichnogo goroda Sanktpeterburga s izobrazheniem znatneishikh onago prospektov, izdannykh trudami imperatorskoi Akademii Nauk i Khudozhestv v Sanktpeterburge.* [St. Petersburg, 1753]. From the collection of Alexander M. Schenker.

Makhaev's view shows the row of symmetrical buildings known as the Twelve Colleges, designed by Trezzini to house the twelve ministries of Peter the Great's administration on Vasilievsky Island (they became part of the University of St. Petersburg in 1819). Begun in 1723, the construction was completed only in the mid-1740s, shortly before Makhaev drew his view. Their unusual orientation, perpendicular to the embankment and facing the eastern tip of the island, is reminiscent of the Place Dauphine on the Ile de la Cité in Paris. The view is evidently taken from Peter the Great's Kunstkammer, historically the first museum of St. Petersburg. The commercial warehouse seen on the right side was replaced in the early nineteenth century by Quarenghi's new exchange bazaar. The canal along the Twelve Colleges was part of the initial plans for Vasilievsky Island (an Amsterdam-like grid of streets and canals). Too narrow, in any event, for commercial navigation, it was subsequently filled in—in its place stands the avenue now called Mendeleevskaia Liniia—, while the empty space in the foreground is now occupied by Quarenghi's 1783–85 building for the Academy of Sciences.

The Petersburg artist M.I. Makhaev (1718–70) drew a series of views of the city which were published in 1753 as a commemorative album to celebrate the fiftieth anniversary of its founding. It comprised a plan of the city, in nine sheets, and twelve plates, engraved by Sokolov, Kachalov, Vinogradov, Vasiliev, Eliakov, and the brothers Vnukov, among others. Unlike some of the early maps of the city, which are idealistic projections into the future, Makhaev's views—some of which come in two parts—are considered the earliest faithful documentation of eighteenth-century St. Petersburg and have proved useful in architectural restoration campaigns.

Mikhail Ivanovich Makhaev. *Vuë de St. Petersbourg. Sur la rivière de Fontancka entre la grotte et le magasin des provisions de la Cour.* Colored engraving after the engraving by G.A. Kachalov. Paris: Basset, undated.

The grotto, which can be seen on the right of Makhaev's view, was a curious edifice begun by the Hamburg architect Andreas Schlüter (the designer of the Charlottenburg Palace in Berlin), who died in 1714, a year after his arrival in St. Petersburg. It was completed by a team of other architects, including Le Blond and Zemtsov. It stood on the western side of the Fontanka and was accessible from the Summer Garden. The baroque structure comprised three rooms connected by arcade-like passages and surmounted by a semicircular cupola. It was decorated with shells and multicolored stones as well as waterworks. At the time Makhaev drew his view, it functioned as a tea room. It was destroyed by the flood that devastated the Summer Garden in 1777.

Another remarkable feature of this view by Makhaev is the depiction of traffic on St. Petersburg's waterways: it shows simple rafts and punts ferrying passengers from one side to the other, luxury barges propelled by ten to twelve oarsmen, and boats used for commercial purposes.

This rather crude copy of Kachalov's engraving is evidence of the popularity enjoyed by Makhaev's views in the eighteenth century.

Vuë de S.ᵗ Petersbourg

Sur la Rivière de Fontancka entre la Grotte et le Magazin des Provisions de la Cour.

Mikhail Ivanovich Makhaev. *Petergofskoi Eia Imperatorskago Velichestva dvorets, na beregu Finlandskago Zaliva v trittsati verstakh ot Sanktpeterburga / Peterhoff, maison de plaisance de Sa Maj.té Imp.le de toutes les Russies &c. &c. &c. Située sur le golfe de Finlande à trente verstes de St. Petersbourg.* From *Résidences de S.M. l'empereur de Russie.* [St. Petersburg, 1761].

General Lieutenant Shubert. *Plan Petergofa i Aleksandrii.* St. Petersburg: Charles Kray, 1842.

In keeping with his admiration for Louis XIV, who built a series of royal residences around Paris, Peter the Great started planning similar residences soon after he founded St. Petersburg. Work started on Peterhof in 1714 on plans by Peter himself, the design being entrusted to Johann Friedrich Braunstein and to Alexandre Le Blond, who expanded the initial conception. In the next ten years, the lower garden, the imperial palace, and the smaller palaces with the revealing names of Marly, Monplaisir, and Hermitage, were built, and the complex was formally inaugurated on 15 August 1723. The most remarkable feature, as can be seen in the 1761 print by Makhaev, is the elaborate system of cascades, sculptures, and waterworks (fed by underground springs on the hill of Ropsha, 14 miles away), which connect the main palace with the lower garden, while symbolizing the victory of Russia over Sweden. The upper garden, behind the imperial palace (no. IV on Lieutenant Shubert's map), was planned but not realized under Peter; it was completed only in the 1730s. During the reign of Elizabeth, Peterhof was considerably modified by her favorite architect, the Paris-born Italian Francesco Bartolomeo Rastrelli (1700–71), whose father, the sculptor and architect Carlo Bartolomeo Rastrelli, had been brought to St. Petersburg by Peter the Great in 1716. To Peterhof he added a third floor and wings terminating with two nearly symmetrical pavillions.

Following his 1753 album on the city proper, Makhaev produced this equally splendid series of five views (three in double plates) of the neighboring imperial residences.

Mikhail Ivanovich Makhaev. *Prospekt Oranienbauma, uveselitelnago dvortsa Eia Imperatorskago
Velichestva pri Finliandskom Zalivie protiv Kronshtata / Vüe d'Oranienbaum maison de plaisance de Sa Majesté
Impériale de toutes les Russies &c. &c. &c. Sur le Golfe de Finlande vis à vis de Cronstadt.* From *Résidences de
S.M. l'empereur de Russie.* [St. Petersburg, 1761].

Oranienbaum—the name (The Orange Tree) is an allusion to the exotic plantings in its original garden—was built between 1710 and 1725 for Alexander Menshikov, Peter the Great's powerful favorite, by the Italian architect Mario Fontana, one of the earliest European architects who worked in St. Petersburg, and the Hamburg-born Gottfried Schädel, who arrived in 1713. Fontana and Schädel erected the main palace, with galleries connecting it to the two large side pavillions, and designed the lower garden in the French style. Rivalling Peterhof in magnificence, the enterprise practically bankrupted Menshikov. At his disgrace in 1727, following the death of Catherine I, the estate became the property of the crown. The view by Makhaev shows the palace as it then stood under the reign of Elizabeth, who gave it in 1743 to her nephew and heir, the future Peter III. It was for him that Rinaldi, in 1756, added a miniature fortress (named Peterstadt), complete with a lake for a miniature navy (this can be seen at the center of the left of the first sheet of Makhaev's view). Catherine the Great commissioned, also from Rinaldi, the much admired Chinese Palace, built in the rococo style and surrounded by a Chinese garden, as well as a glissoire, of which only the main pavillion survives.

Mikhail Ivanovich Makhaev. *Dvorets Eia Imperatorskago Velichestva v Sarskom Sele v 25. ti verstakh ot Sanktpeterburga / Maison de plaisance de Sa Maj.té Imp.le de toutes les Russies &c. &c. &c. à Sarskoe Selo, 25 verstes de St. Petersbourg.* From *Résidences de S.M. l'empereur de Russie.* [St. Petersburg, 1761].

General Lieutenant Shubert. *Plan goroda Tsarskago-Sela.* St. Petersburg: Charles Kray, 1844.

The first palace in Tsarskoe Selo ("The Tsar's Village") was built under Catherine I and it is after her that it is known as the Catherine Palace. Immediately upon her accession, her daughter Elizabeth resolved to transform it and employed several architects to that effect, but it was only in 1752 that Rastrelli was entrusted with the task of redoing and unifying the whole. The work was completed in 1756. As can be seen in Makhaev's near contemporary picture of the finished palace, Rastrelli incorporated the earlier structure, flanking it with two wings of approximately the same height. At the end of the wings were two pavillions, one, containing the royal chapel, surmounted by five cupolas, the other surmounted by a star, symbol of Elizabeth. To gain access to the empress, visitors had to go through an enfilade of spectacular rooms, culminating in the great hall, modelled on the Galerie des Glaces in Versailles.

Rastrelli also rearranged the grounds and built several pavillions in the park. Makhaev's print shows the other side, the formal cour d'honneur, in which Elizabeth can be seen, accompanied by her ladies in waiting, entering her palace in an imposing litter drawn by twenty horses.

Catherine the Great modified Tsarskoe Selo further, employing mostly the Italian architect Antonio Rinaldi (1709–90), who moved to Russia in 1751 and remained there for three decades. He redesigned the park of Tsarskoe Selo as a vast allegory of Catherine's victorious campaigns against the Turks — the intended ambition of which was the conquest of Constantinople.

The Shubert map shows subsequent additions made under Catherine and her successors: Quarenghi's Alexander Palace (45), the Imperial Lyceum, where Pushkin was a student (121), and the railroad and train station (148). Inaugurated in 1836, but opened only the following year, the line connecting the capital to Tsarskoe Selo was the first in Russia. The train station in St. Petersburg was, in fact, called the Tsarskoe Selo Station; it was renamed Vitebskii Vokzal (Vitebsk Station) after the Revolution.

Ezra Stiles. Holograph draft of a letter to Benjamin Franklin.
Newport, 20 February 1765.

Benjamin Franklin. Autograph letter, signed, to Ezra Stiles. London,
5 July 1765.

As Eufrosina Dvoichenko-Markoff has pointed out, the name of Benjamin Franklin is
closely associated with the beginnings of American-Russian cultural relations in the
eighteenth century, because of his contacts with the Imperial Academy of Sciences in
St. Petersburg, the institution founded by Peter the Great in 1718, though it opened
only in 1725, shortly after his death. These contacts are evidenced by the letter Ezra
Stiles, the future president of Yale College, wrote to Franklin from Newport on 20
February 1765, a retained copy of which is preserved in the former's papers. Stiles asks
Franklin to forward a scientific memorandum on thermometrical matters (known in a
Latin copy at the American Philosophical Society) to Mikhail Vasilievich Lomonosov
(1711–65), the greatest Russian scientist of his age — as well as its greatest poet.
Lomonosov, who became professor of chemistry at the University of St. Petersburg,
had been involved in Georg Wilhelm Richmann's experiments in atmospheric
electricity and barely survived one of them in 1753, in the course of which Richmann
himself was fatally struck by lightning. Stiles suggests that his memorandum to
Lomonosov might interest Franklin himself; this could explain the presence of a copy
at the American Philosophical Society. It is in Latin, which was presumably the
language Stiles used to communicate with his Russian colleagues. The letter also
mentions the names of two prominent German-born members of the Petersburg
Academy: the physician Franz Ulrich Theodor Aepinus (1724–1802), who became
tutor to Tsarevich Paul, and "Braunius," a.k.a. Josef Adam Braun (1712–68), professor
of philosophy at the University of St. Petersburg, who first achieved the solidification
of mercury. In addition, Stiles conveys to Franklin his interest in the expedition to the
Arctic Ocean that was about to be launched from Russia to find a northeast passage to
the East Indies. The expedition left from Archangel in May 1765 but was unsuccessful.

In his response, dated 5 July, Franklin promises to forward to Lomonosov Stiles's
memorandum. Lomonosov, however, had died on 4 April, a fact of which Franklin
was evidently unaware.

Franklin had subsequent contacts with two other prominent members of the
Imperial Academy, Prince Dmitrii Alekseevich Golitsyn (1734–1803), and Ekaterina
Romanovna Dashkova (1744–1810), née Vorontsova, who combined her scientific and
literary pursuits with the functions of lady-in-waiting to Catherine the Great (having
participated in the plot which brought her to power), and became director of the
Imperial Academy in 1782. She and Franklin met in Paris in 1781. Eight years later, she
was elected a member of the American Philosophical Society, while Franklin himself
became a member of the Imperial Academy on 2 November 1789. Two days later,
Princess Dashkova conveyed the news to him in a charming letter which she wrote
directly in English. The original has apparently not survived, but it is quoted in William
Temple Franklin's *Memoirs of the life and writings of Benjamin Franklin* (1818): "Dear Sir,
having always supposed, and even cherished the idea, that you were a member of the
Imperial Academy of Sciences, which is at St. Petersburgh under my direction, I was
greatly surprised, when reviewing the list of its members some days ago, I did not find
your name in the number. I hastened therefore to acquire this honor for the academy,
and you were received among its members with unanimous applause and joy. I beg
you, Sir, to accept this title, and to believe that I look upon it as an honor acquired by
our academy." Six months later, the Imperial Academy was mourning the death of its
first American member.

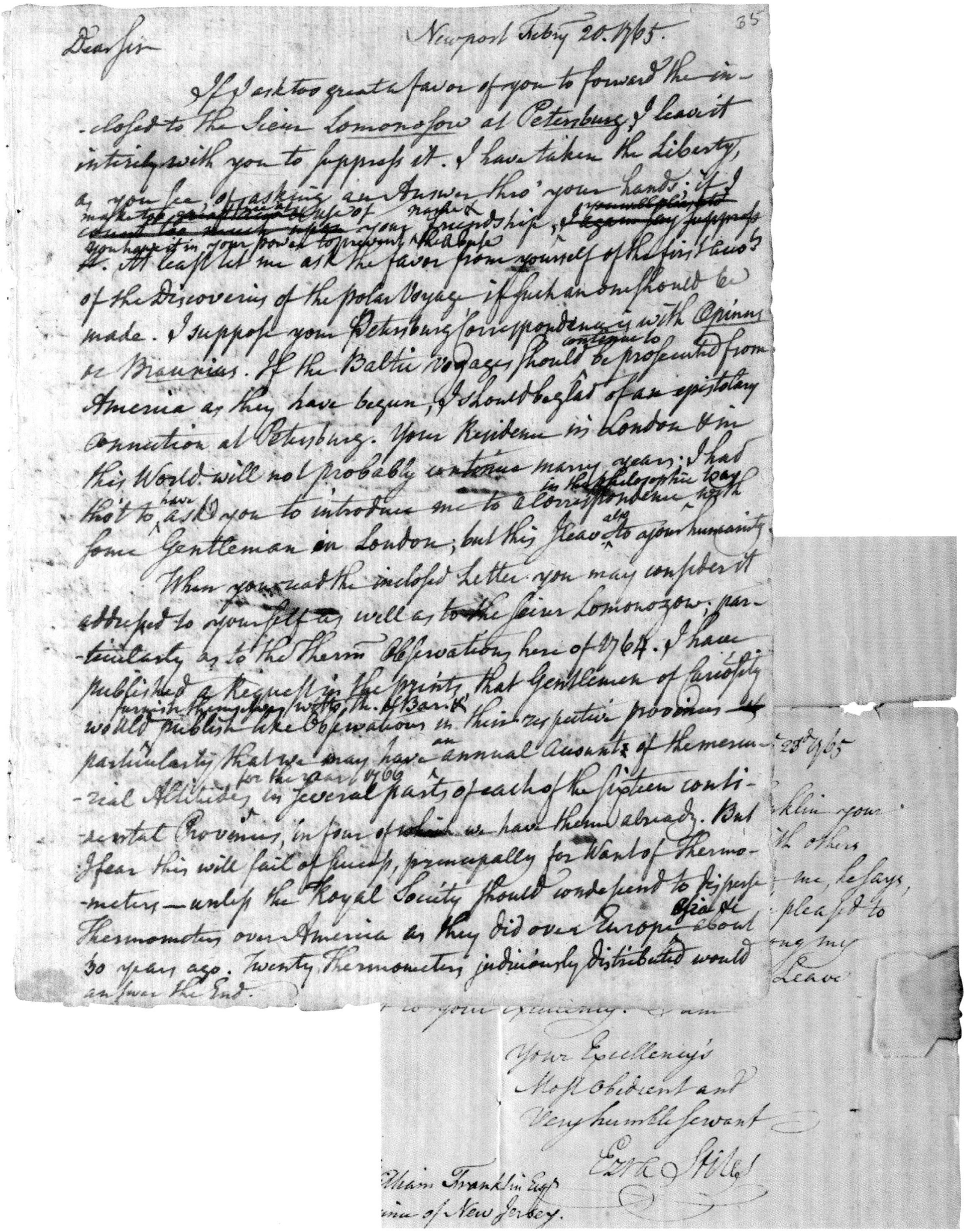

Dear Sir   Newport Febry 20. 1765.

If I ask too great a favor of you to forward the inclosed to the Sieur Lomonosow at Petersburg, I leave it
intirely with you to suppress it. I have taken the Liberty,
as you see, of asking an Answer thro' your hands: If I
~~make too~~ ~~consent the doubt upon~~ your ~~friendship,~~ ^would please^
~~you have it in your power to prevent the abuse~~ ~~I again say suppress~~
~~it.~~ At least let me ask the favor from yourself of the first & news
of the discoveries of the polar Voyage if such an one should be
made. I suppose your Petersburg Correspondence is with Ӕpinus
or Braunius. If the Baltic Voyages should ^continue to^ be prosecuted from
America as they have begun, I should be glad of an epistolary
Connection at Petersburg. Your Residence in London & in
this World will not probably continue many years: I had
tho't to ^have^ ask'd you to introduce me to a Correspondence ^in the philosophic way^ with
some ^Gentleman^ in London; but this I leave ^also^ to ^your humanity^.

When you read the inclosed Letter you may consider it
addressed to ^yourself^ as well as to ~~the~~ Sieur Lomonosow, particularly as to the therm Observations here of 1764. I have
published a Request in the prints, that Gentlemen of Curiosity
would ^furnish themselves with the Barom^ publish like Observations in their respective provinces —
particularly that we may have ^an^ annual Account of the mercu-
rial Altitudes ^for the year 1765^ in several parts of each of the sixteen continental Provinces, in four of ~~which~~ we have them already. But
I fear this will fail of success, principally for Want of thermometers — unless the Royal Society should condescend to dispense
Thermometers over America as they did over Europe ^about^ ^30 years ago^. Twenty Thermometers judiciously distributed would
answer the End.

                    to your Excellency.   I am

                              Your Excellency's
                              Most Obedient and
                              Very humble Servant
                                        Ezra Stiles

William Franklin Esqr
of New Jersey.

Dear Sir   London July 5.th 1765

I received your very ingenious Letter of February 20.th
and shall shortly forward that which was enclos'd for Lomonozow.—

You need not have made any Apology for sending it thro' my hands,
as if you gave me Trouble. When I can do any thing to Oblige you, it is a
Pleasure.

Your Remarks on the Coldness of Snow are curious. It seems
that a Degree of heat heigher than 32 cannot be given to it all
above that going off in melted water and that it does not usually begin
to thaw, till the whole has receiv'd that Degree. But a greater
Degree of Cold may be given as the Snow is fixt to abide it.—

Thro' probably the increas'd Coldness of the Air is not suddenly
communicated to the Body of Snow, but requir's some time to make
it equally cold.

I think that in some of the Petersburg Experiments of freezing
Mercury, part of the ☿ was left in the Tube, so that when the
Glass was broke, there appear'd a solid Ball connected to a Silver
Wire. If so their Thermometers were such as you would have used.

As my time here is uncertain, and much taken up in other
Affairs, so that I can have little Attention to Philos-
-ophical Matters, I shall indeavour to get D.r Watson to corresp
with you.

I never saw the Account in the News paper of the intend
-ed Polar Voyage by the Rusians which you Mention, and
I doubt there is some Miftake in it.—The Rusians have made
two Voyags to the Northwest Part of America from the North East
Part Afia;—but all their Attempts of going round by the North
Sea have faild. One Ship was fix'd fast in the Ice by the extream
Cold 40 Miles from Land and the men quitted her and Walked
ashore.—However Lomonozow will set the Matter right.

I have lately propos'd our ingenious & learned Contriman
M.r Winthorp, as a Member of the Royal Society.—He can not
be Chosen, according to the Rules, till some time in December next
as the Society is adjourn'd. You need not mention it to him
till it is compleat. This I have obserd in your Case with
Regard to the Doctorate I procur'd for you. I first engag'd a
Friend, M.r Strahan of this City, to propose it in a Letter to
some friend of his at Edinburgh. He accordingly wrote to D.r
Robertson (the Historian) who was a Friend of mine & made
                                        Principal

University since I was in Scotland, which I had
ould have apply'd to him directly. I
y of his Answer to M.r Strahan, my Letter
r to me, & my Reply—that you may see how
s acted. They are all in the Tin Box with the
will be right for you to send a short Latin
the University, which if it comes to any Hands
transmit. I wish you Joy of the Honour don
ould not have recommended you if I had not
would prove an Honour to the University that confer

l Letter from D.r Robertson to me, be pleas'd
after perusal, to be put among my Papers

ber me affectionately to Gov.r Ward and all
amily. With sincerest Esteem.
Friend

Yours affectionately

B Franklin

Francesco, Conte Algarotti. *Lettres du comte Algarotti sur la Russie, contenant l'état du commerce, de la marine, des revenus, & des forces de cet empire: avec l'histoire de la guerre de 1735 contre les Turcs, & des observations sur la mer Baltique, & la mer Caspienne. Traduites de l'italien.* London and Paris: Merlin, 1769.

The young Venetian scientist, author of *Il Neutonianismo per le dame* (eventually retitled *Dialoghi sopra l'ottica neutoniana*), visited Russia in the summer of 1739. His account of his trip was first published in Paris, as *Viaggi di Russia*, in 1760. It was written in the form of eight letters to Lord Hervey, dated from 10 June 1739 to 30 September 1739. An augmented edition appeared in 1763, also in Paris: it comprised four additional letters to the playwright and scholar Scipione Maffei, dated from 27 August 1750 to 24 August 1751, and dealing mostly with the English trade through Russia and the area surrounding the Caspian Sea.

Four of the letters to Hervey are dated from the St. Petersburg area. The third letter describes Kronshtadt and discusses Peter the Great's will to make Russia a naval power. It is at the beginning of the fourth letter, dated from St. Petersburg proper (as are the following two), that Algarotti describes the city as "that great window, lately opened in the North, through which Russia looks towards Europe," a phrase quoted at the beginning of Pushkin's poem *The Bronze Horseman*, with due attribution to Algarotti in the accompanying notes. It is likely that Pushkin read Algarotti in this French edition.

This inspired metaphor notwithstanding, Algarotti's account of the city is mixed. He contrasts the splendor of its appearance seen from afar with the drabness of its location and the perpetually crumbling state of the palaces, while noting that the main edifices are hardly the work of Inigo Joneses or Palladios.

Algarotti later occupied diplomatic functions at the courts of Frederick II and August III of Saxony and wrote important critical studies of architecture and painting.

(64)

LETTRE IV.

Au même.

De St. Pétersbourg le 30 Juin 1739.

JE n'ai pas de plus grand plaisir, Mylord, que de vous écrire; & je le fais le plus souvent qu'il m'est possible. Je vais enfin vous parler de cette nouvelle ville, de cette grande fenêtre, ouverte récemment dans le Nord, par où la Russie regarde en Europe. Nous sommes arrivés à St. Pétersbourg, ces jours derniers, après en avoir passé deux à Cronstadt, chez l'Amiral Gordon : nous y avons laissé notre frégate, qui, prenant onze pieds d'eau, n'auroit pu remonter au-delà de Péterhoff; & nous nous sommes rendus ici, dans une barque aussi belle que bien décorée, que nous a donnée l'Amiral.

Sept mois de l'année on voyage sur

Benoît-Louis Henriquez. Engraving of the head of the equestrian statue of Peter the Great for the equestrian statue by Étienne Falconet, after Anton Pavlovich Losenko. St. Petersburg, 1772. From the collection of Alexander M. Schenker.

Soon after her accession to power in 1762, Catherine II decided to erect a monument to Peter the Great. Bids were solicited in France, through the offices of the Russian minister in Paris, Prince Dmitrii Alekseevich Golitsyn. On the strength of Denis Diderot's recommendation to Catherine, the commission was awarded in 1766 to the 50-year-old Étienne Falconet, a close friend of the philosophe, who was then employed by the royal porcelain manufacture of Sèvres. Falconet left Paris in August of that year, accompanied by his 18-year-old pupil, Marie-Anne Collot (who was probably his mistress, even though she eventually married his son in 1777). The head of the statue was credited to her by Falconet himself, but it is probable that he participated in it.

Falconet's twelve-year stay in St. Petersburg was marked by constant frictions with the overseer of the project, General Ivan Ivanovich Betskoi, director of the Bureau of Imperial Buildings and Gardens and president of the Academy of Fine Arts. The sculptor, however, for the first five years of his stay at least, enjoyed the empress's protection and was able to appeal directly to her.

Work on the large model for the monument began in February 1768 and was completed in August 1769. The model was publicly exhibited in the summer of 1770 and caused a sensation. Falconet's realistic depiction of a horse in movement, in the face of classical traditions of equestrian representation exemplified by the statue of Marcus Aurelius on the Piazza del Campidoglio in Rome, triggered a polemic in which the sculptor took a firm stance against his Roman predecessor. An anonymous attack in Baron Grimm's *Correspondance littéraire,* which the sculptor had good reasons to believe emanated from Diderot, provoked the end of their friendship in 1773, just as the philosophe was about to arrive in St. Petersburg at the personal invitation of Catherine, with

whom Falconet's relations had by then badly deteriorated.

After several years of fruitless search for an appropriate caster, Falconet decided to take the responsibility himself. A first attempt partially failed in August 1775, unleashing a new polemic involving one of the workers responsible for baking the mold. Nearly two years later, in July 1777, the second casting was a success, and by the end of the year the statue was ready to be installed. In August 1778, Falconet left Russia. Catherine the Great had yet to see the completed statue; she did not respond to Falconet's final letter, nor did she receive him before his departure.

The installing of the monument was supervised by the architect Iurii Matveevich Fel'ten (originally Georg Friedrich Velten, the nephew of Peter the Great's German chef). The snake which Peter tramples with his horse was realized, after Falconet's design, by Fedor Gordeevich Gordeev. The unveiling took place on 7 August 1782 with great solemnity, marking the centenary of Peter the Great's coronation.

Falconet, who had returned to Paris, was about to undertake his first trip to Italy in 1783 when he suffered a massive stroke. He died in 1791. Widowed shortly afterwards, Collot retired to Lorraine and died in Nancy in 1821.

The technical accomplishment and power of the Bronze Horseman, as Falconet's statue has come to be known, have made it not only one of the greatest monuments ever created, but the very symbol of St. Petersburg. No one has expressed it more vividly than Pushkin in his 1833 poem, published only (and incompletely) after his death, and set in the context of the catastrophic 1824 flood. Evgeny, the young hero of the poem, reduced to poverty and despair after losing his house and his fiancée in the disaster, hurls a curse at the statue, which, as he imagines it, starts chasing him through the streets of the city.

TÊTE DE LA STATUE ÉQUESTRE
DE
PIERRE LE GRAND.

Maria Anna Collot fecit. Antonius Lossinko delineavit. Benedictus Ludovicus Henriquez Sculpsit Petropoli 1772.

Marinos Charbourès [Marin Carburi]. *Monument élevé à la gloire de Pierre-le-Grand, ou relation des travaux et des moyens méchaniques qui ont été employés pour transporter à Pétersbourg un rocher de trois millions pesant, destiné à servir de base à la statue équestre de cet empereur; avec un examen physique et chymique du même rocher.* Paris: Nyon aîné; Stoupe, 1777.

An unusual feature of Falconet project from the outset was that the equestrian statue of Peter was to stand on a naked rock rather than on a conventional pedestal decorated with bas-relief representations of some of the tsar's victories and achievements. The first challenge was to find a rock large enough for the enterprise. The search was undertaken under the supervision of Betskoi's Greek-born aide-de-camp, Captain Marin Carburi (1729–82). Carburi was a somewhat shady figure who had been forced to leave Venice in 1759 after slashing the face of a woman who resisted his advances. While in Russia, he adorned himself with the spurious title of Chevalier de Lascaris and, as A. M. Schenker has suggested, he may have done some intelligence work for the Venetian Republic.

In September 1768, a suitable granite boulder was located in a marshy, woody area off the shore of the Gulf of Finland, about eight miles from St. Petersburg as the crow flies. By February 1769, the rock had been excavated. The second challenge, to which Carburi, a trained engineer, rose magnificently, was to transport the rock, first from its site to the coast, then by boat to the spot where the statue was to stand. Carburi devised a complex machinery, first to lift the 3-million-pound boulder from the ground, install it on a platform, and transfer it to a chassis which, supported by encased metal balls, was rolled five miles downhill to the large pier especially built in the Bay of Kronshtadt. An initial attempt failed in April 1769; the long process was accomplished between mid-November 1769 and the end of March 1770.

A large raft was constructed especially for the transportation of the rock across the Gulf of Finland. In August 1770, the rock was pulled on the barge, not without further delays and complications. Finally, the barge docked and by mid-October the base of the statue was installed on Senate Square. The astonishing engineering feat was celebrated across Europe in a way that A. M. Schenker has likened to the publicity surrounding the launching of the first sputnik in 1957.

Carburi, who did not lack enemies, fell out of favor soon afterwards and in 1773 left for Paris, where he published his account of the transportation of the rock in this handsome commemorative volume, illustrated with twelve folding plates by D'Elvaux and Sellier after Blarenberghe and Fossier. The physical and chemical description of the rock, which follows the account of its transportation, is the work of Carburi's brother Jean-Baptiste, a physician, who taught medicine at the universities of Paris and Turin, and was a consultant to King Louis XVI and his younger brother the Count of Artois, the future Charles X.

Carburi himself was stabbed to death in 1782 by disgruntled Morean workers on the American-style plantation he had started developing on his native island of Cephalonia.

Pl. VIII.

Echelle

5   10   15   20   25   30 pieds.

ÉTAT PRÉSENT

DE LA

RUSSIE.

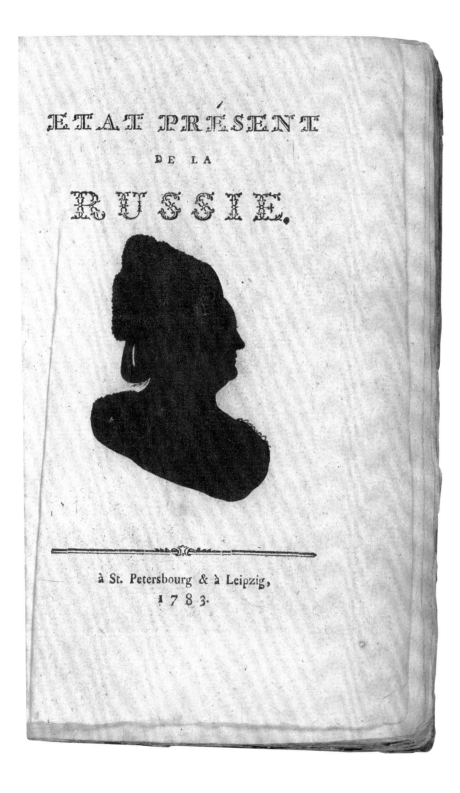

à St. Petersbourg & à Leipzig,
1783.

Pieter van Woensel. *État présent de la Russie.* St. Petersburg and Leipzig, 1783.

The author of this anonymous memoir was a Dutch physician, born in 1747 and trained in Leiden, who subsequently moved to St. Petersburg, where he held medical positions with the general hospital for the infantry and with the Land Cadets Corps, the institution founded by Empress Anne in 1731 for the education of young noblemen. His publications include an abridgement of Abbé Raynal's *Histoire philosophique et politique de l'établissement et du commerce des Européens dans les deux Indes,* published in Amsterdam (in French) in 1762; a memoir on the plague, printed in the Russian capital in 1788; a tract reporting on experiments with mercury in treating the small pox, published under the auspices of the Royal Society of Medicine in Paris; and a two-volume account of travels through Turkey, Anatolia, and Crimea during the years 1784–89, which came out in Dutch, in Constantinople, in 1791–94. He died in 1808.

Woensel's *De tegenwoordige staat van Rusland* was first published in Amsterdam in 1781. This French version was produced, and somewhat adapted, from the German translation which was issued, also in St. Petersburg, the following year. The French translator, in addition to supplying some footnotes from the German edition, added peculiar footnotes of his own ("Only a doctor would write like this" etc.).

As he explains in his preface, Woensel, by 1781, had spent more than six years in Russia. His précis, which is largely a description of St. Petersburg, contains an interesting portrait of Catherine II, whose silhouette head appears on the title page. "One need not be a Lavater," writes our doctor, "to judge that such a handsome physiognomy reveals the most sensitive heart and the most enlightened spirit . . . Her passions are strong, and that can probably extend to vehemence. She has a solid judgement, intuition, strength of mind; she is devoid of prejudices generally, and particularly of those of her sex." There are, in no particular order, short chapters on the court, the Winter Palace ("Almost all travellers find it unsatisfactory because of its size and uniformity"), the Hermitage and its collections, the Summer Palace, the Academy of Sciences and its members, the Imperial Library and Kunstkammer, the Academy of Fine Arts, music, the education system, the sciences, medicine, private collectors, and so on. Chapter XXXIX, one of the longest, is devoted to a description of St. Petersburg, including an interesting account of Vasilievsky Island, the Palace Embankment ("the most beautiful place in the city"), Admiralty Prospect, and the three canals. The following chapter deals with the statue of Peter the Great, which was still not in place when Woensel was writing ("Everything having been ready for a long time, it is inconceivable what may postpone the erection of this monument") but was completed by the time the translation appeared, as a note from the translator makes clear. Woensel's enthusiastic account both of the statue and of the transportation of its rocky pedestal (although he mistranscribes the inscription) is revealing of the excitement generated by Falconet's work.

The remaining chapters survey other noteworthy aspects of the city and its surroundings, including the imperial palaces. Then follow an account of the government and administration and a short history of Russia. The final chapter, "Horoscope of Russia," ends with a plea for the abolition of serfdom.

"There is every appearance," Woensel writes of St. Petersburg, "that in two centuries this will be the first city of the universe."

Fabbriche e disegni di Giacomo Quarenghi architetto di S.M. l'imperatore di Russia, cavaliere di Malta e di S. Walodimiro, illustrate dal Cav. Giulio suo figlio.
Mantua: Negretti, 1843.

In 1778, Catherine the Great wrote to Grimm that she was looking for new architects and was hoping to find them in Italy, since St. Petersburg was full of Frenchmen who knew too much and only built unsatisfactory houses. Her major contribution to the evolution of St. Petersburg architecture was the recruitment, the following year, of Giacomo Quarenghi (1744–1817), representative and advocate of a strict neoclassical style.

Born in Bergamo, trained in Rome, Quarenghi signed his contract in September 1779 and remained in St. Petersburg for the rest of his life. He had fallen under the spell of Palladio as a student and never deviated from his master's principles. No other architect had more influence on the exterior appearance of the city, to the point where his buildings, or those inspired by his style, have become identified with its general architectural tone.

The buildings illustrated in the commemorative volume published in 1821 in Milan and reissued in Mantua in 1843 (with a new dedication to the future Alexander II) convey the number and range of Quarenghi's St. Petersburg commissions: the Alexander Palace in Tsarskoe Selo; the Imperial Horseguards Manège on St. Isaac's Square; the Institute for the Education of Noble Girls in the Smolny Monastery; the Gagarin Palace on the Neva; the gallery in the Sheremetev Palace; the Hermitage Theater; the Vestibule to the French Gallery in the Hermitage; the chapel for the Order of Malta (of which Paul I had himself appointed Grand Master) in the Vorontsov Palace; the English Pavillion at Peterhof; merchant galleries ("Botteghe") near the Kunstkammer ("Palazzo del gabinetto imperiale"); the hospital named after Tsarina Maria Feodorovna; the triumphal arch in honor of Alexander I; the Imperial Bank on Sadovaia Street; the Observatory; the Iusupov Palace on the Fontanka; more merchant galleries on Vasilievsky Island; the coffee-house and cold baths at Tsarskoe Selo; and the English Reformed Church on the English Embankment, Quarenghi's last project, completed only after his death.

The Hermitage Theater (1785–87), with its semi-circular auditorium, inspired by ancient models and Palladio's own reconstitution in Vicenza, was particularly admired. Quarenghi was recompensed with lodgings in the same building, which he occupied until his death. (Plays written by Catherine herself were staged in the Hermitage Theater.)

The volume also documents unrealized projects, such as a concert hall at Tsarskoe Selo and a large theater in St. Petersburg.

The Hermitage Theater, by Sadovnikov (ca. 1833).

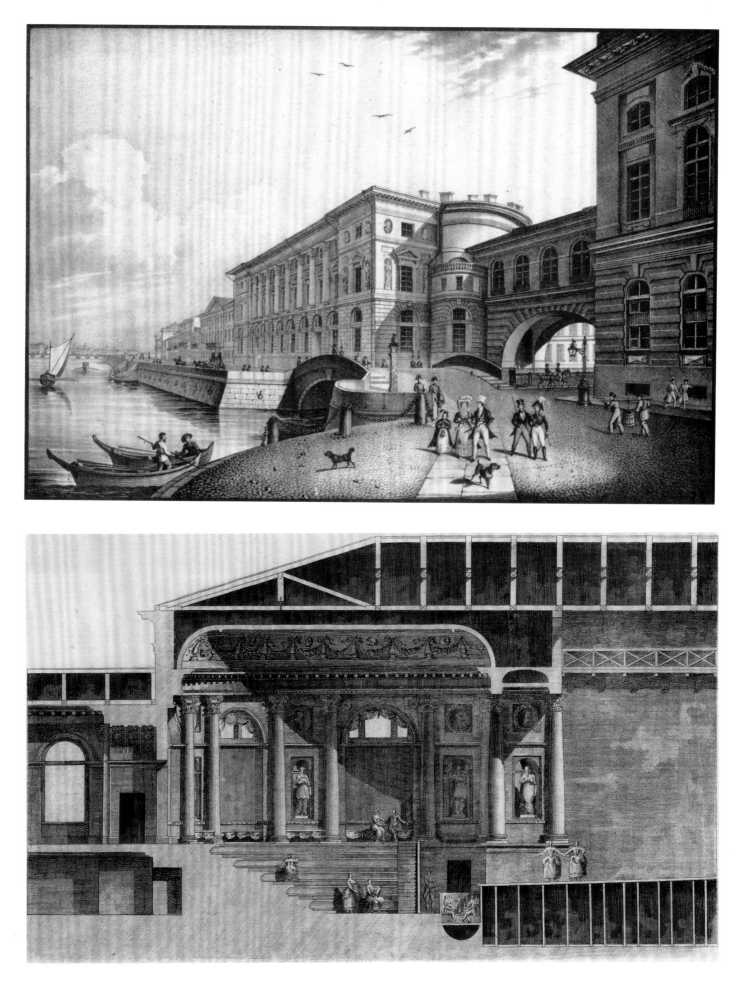

Lithograph by Langlumé after Bichebois (1822), entitled "Une journée à Pawlosky," from Dupré de Sainte-Maure's *Anthologie russe* (1823).

General Lieutenant Shubert. *Plan Pavlovska.* St. Petersburg: Charles Kray, 1842.

Vasilii Semenovich Sadovnikov. *Vid sniatyi v Pavlovskom Parke / Vue prise dans le parc de Pavlovsky.*
Lithograph by Ivanov. From *Kostiumy i vidy St. Peterburga i okrestnosti. Souvenir de St. Petersbourg.* Paris: H.
Prévost, 1833.

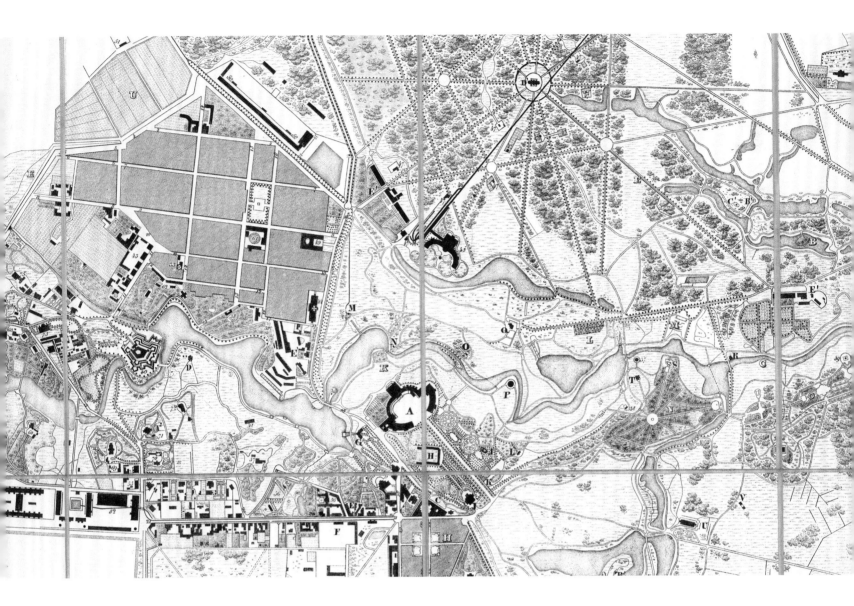

The Pavlovsk estate was a gift from Catherine II to her son, the future Paul I, in honor of the birth of his son, the future Alexander I, in 1777. The palace and park, and several of the various pavillions that grace the latter, were built and designed between 1781 and 1786 by the Scottish architect Charles Cameron (ca. 1743–1812). Trained in Rome like Quarenghi, Cameron, like him also, arrived in St. Petersburg in 1779. His first major work was the Agate Room at Tsarskoe Selo.

As can be seen on the plan drawn in the 1840s by Lieutenant Shubert (himself a resident of the Pavlovsk village), the palace proper (A) is in the shape of a classic Palladian villa flanked by two semi-circular wings. The park, a vast English garden, is ornamented with neoclassical monuments, such as the Temple of Friendship (P) and Apollo Colonnade (M), some of which can be seen in Sadovnikov's view.

Pavlovsk is inseparable from the memory of Empress Maria Feodorovna (1759–1828), born Sophia of Württemberg, the second wife of Paul I, who greatly embellished it after his death in 1801. Its romantic park was influenced by the one at Chantilly, which the future tsar and his wife, travelling as Comte and Comtesse du Nord, had admired during their Grand Tour in the early 1780s.

à St: Petersbourg le 8 Mai 1789. v. 11.
reçu le 2 Juin

Monsieur mon très-cher et très-honoré Oncle,

Il y a déjà 10 jours que je Vous dois une réponse à Votre chère et agréable lettre du 25
avril, mais je voulus attendre que les noces fussent passées, pourque ma lettre devint
un peu plus intéressante. Les Dames Behmer attendent toujours la decision de leur
sort qui de rechef devient douteuse. Si elles obtiennent le renouvellement de leur ferme
elles pourront encore passer une année ici, si on le leur refuse, elles retourneront
tous de suite et en droiture à Beiscastel. Si Vous avez appris quelque chose
à Berlin de Mlle. Daron je Vous prie de m'en faire part: elle me paroit un
peu timbrée, et avoir quelques fois des rèves. L'autre jour elle soutint à ma
femme que M. de Doffow lui a fait des propositions de l'épouser, elle en a même
fait l'ouverture à la Comtesse Pouschkien, et M. de Doffow la deteste. Elle
assure aussi que la Comtesse Pouschkien lui a promis 2000 roubles et qu'elle
lui en fera encore avoir de S. M. 2000 rôb. et la Comtesse Pouschkien m'a
assuré que l'idée ne lui en est pas venue. Enfin j'en voudrois bien être
debarassé. — Aller en Russie signifie à St. Petersbourg, partir ou s'établir
dans l'intérieur du Pais. — L'Amiral Paul Jones est encore ici, mais
il est à une espèce d'inquisition, pour avoir fait un enfant à une fille
de dix ans. Il a beau proferer des certificats des Chirurgiens qu'il est
impuissant, il a beau prouver que la mere lui a livré la fille pour une
Somme d'argent, et que toute fois il n'a fait que badiner avec cet enfans; on croit toujours qu'on finira par lui oter le cordon de Ste.
Anne et de le chasser. On n'auroit jamais du lui donner ni titre
ni cordon. Je souhaite à Monsieur Votre fils toute la satisfaction qu'il
se promet du voyage qu'il va entreprendre: il ne manquera pas d'être le
très bien reçu par tout où il se présentera — mais pourquoi ne vou-
droit-il pas faire aussi un tour à St. Petersbourg? Ce feroit une bien
grande consolation pour nous que de voir encore un des Vôtres. Notre
Académie a aussi reçu la notification de la mort de Pierre Camper,
Elle a perdu depuis le commencement de cette année trois de ses
membres externes, Lyonet, d'Holbach et Camper. Hebenstreit à
Leipzig dois aussi être mort, mais je ne me rappelle pas en avoir
lu dans les journeaux litteraires une indice plus particulière.
Votre lettre est toute intéressante d'un bout à l'autre: je l'ai relu
toujours avec le plus grand plaisir, et j'aurois encore bien de
choses à Vous dire et bien des matieres à m'entretenir avec Vous.
                                                    mais

Johann Albrecht Euler. Autograph letter, signed, to his uncle. St. Petersburg, 8 May 1789.

The physicist J.A. Euler (1734–1800) writes to his uncle in Berlin. After some witty local gossip, Euler notes that "in St. Petersburg, to go to Russia means to go or settle in the interior of the country." He then reports the current scandal affecting John Paul Jones who, following his American revolutionary war exploits, had received from Catherine the Great a commission as rear admiral to fight in the war she had just declared on the Ottoman Empire. "Admiral Paul Jones," writes Euler, "is still here, but he is at a kind of inquisition for having gotten a girl of ten years of age pregnant. Even though he produced certificates from surgeons that he is impotent and proved that the mother turned the girl over to him for a sum of money, and that in any event he only bantered with that child, it is still believed that his decoration of St. Anne will be taken away from him and he will be expelled. He should never have been given title or decoration." Jones's guilt is still a matter of dispute among historians. Allowed by

Catherine to leave Russia in July 1789, he settled in Paris, just as the French Revolution was getting underway, and died there five years later.

The remainder of the letter mentions the deaths of three external members of the Imperial Academy of Sciences: the Dutch physician Petrus Camper (1722–89), the French naturalist Pierre Lyonnet (1702–89), and the German materialist philosopher Paul-Henri Thiry, baron d'Holbach, born in 1723, who actually did not die until 21 June. He concludes by mentioning that the empress is curious to know about a gnomonic instrument that had been sent to the Academy two years previously: "this is going to keep me busy until dinner time."

Elder son of the great Swiss mathematician and physicist Leonhard Euler (1707–83), Johann Albrecht followed his father to St. Petersburg and became himself a member of the Imperial Academy in 1766.

Enea nel Lazio: Opera in due Atti con balli analoghi da rappresentarsi nell'Imperial Teatro di Gatchina in occasione delle faustissime nozze di Sua Altezza Imperiale La Gran Duchessa Elena Pavlovna con Sua Altezza Serenissima Federico Luigi Principe Ereditario di Meckenbourg-Schwerin. St. Petersburg: Imperial Press, 1799.

A century before Verdi received the commission to write *La forza del destino* for the Imperial Theater, St. Petersburg already had an Italian opera company and Italian composers in residence. In 1757, the impresario and librettist Giovanni Battista Locatelli (1713–ca. 1790) moved from Prague to Russia to become director of Elizabeth's opera company, bringing Italian singers and introducing Italian works to the Russian capital. In his troupe was the castrato Manfredini, whose brother Vincenzo (1737–99) became maestro di cappella to the future Peter III. Manfredini's opera seria *Semiramide riconosciuta* was performed at Oranienbaum in 1760, while his pastorale *La musica trionfante* was given the following year in St. Petersburg. When he ascended the throne in 1762, Peter III appointed Manfredini music director of the imperial Italian opera company. Two years later, Catherine II brought to Russia the more famous Venetian composer Baldassare Galuppi (1706–85), then one of the most performed operatic composers, who occupied the positions of maestro di coro at the Basilica of San Marco and the Ospedale degli Incurabili. Galuppi became music director, while Manfredini produced ballets (*Les amants réchappés du naufrage* and *Le sculpteur de Carthage*, both performed in St. Petersburg in 1766). In addition to the operas he wrote or revived in Russia (the most important new work being *Ifigenia in Tauride*), Galuppi composed choral works based on Russian texts for the Orthodox liturgy. He returned to Venice, where he was visited in 1782 by Tsarevich Paul. As for Manfredini, who had been Paul's harpsichord teacher, he had returned to Italy in 1769 but was invited back to St. Petersburg by his imperial pupil in 1798 and died there a year later.

Galuppi was succeeded by Tommaso Traetta (1727–79). Born in Puglia, near Bari, Traetta was trained in Naples and occupied a court appointment in Parma, achieving fame with operas premiered in Mannheim and Vienna. He was director of the music conservatory of the Ospedaletto in Venice when he was recruited by the court of St. Petersburg, where he arrived in late 1768. His opera *Antigone* was premiered in the Russian capital in 1772. He returned to Venice three years later.

The next Italian maestro di cappella was the Neapolitan Giovanni Paisiello (1740–1816), who was in residence in St. Petersburg from the summer of 1776 until 1783. It was under his tenure that the Imperial Opera Company's ban on opere buffe was lifted in 1779. In addition to writing operas for the company (among them *Il Barbiere di Siviglia*, after Beaumarchais's 1776 comedy, premiered at the Hermitage Theater in 1782), Paisiello was the harpsichord teacher of Maria Feodorovna, the second wife of the future Paul I. It was at the latter's suggestion that Catherine II recruited Giuseppe Sarti (1729–1802) to succeed Paisiello. Sarti was then maestro di cappella at the Milan cathedral and the author of several popular stage works, including *Fra i due litiganti il terzo gode*, which Mozart quotes in the final scene of *Don Giovanni*.

Sarti's *Enea nel Lazio*, "opera in due atti con balli analoghi," given at the palace of Gatchina for the wedding of Grand Duchess Elena, daughter of Paul I, is a characteristic example of the lavish entertainment provided by the St. Petersburg Italian composers. The libretto, based on the tragedy by Carlo Goldoni, itself inspired by books VII–XII of the *Aeneid*, is interspersed with two ballets, "Il sogno di Enea" and "Feste dei popoli dal Lazio," in which French and Russian dancers were led by Charles Lepick (1744?–1806), a disciple of Noverre, who was ballet master in St. Petersburg since 1786; his wife Gertrude, a famous ballerina, was, from a previous marriage, the mother of the architect Carlo Rossi. She appeared as Venus in *Enea nel Lazio*.

Among the other works Sarti wrote in St. Petersburg was a Russian opera, *Nachal'noie upravlenie Olega* (The early reign of Oleg) on a libretto by Catherine II, who was also involved in the production in 1790. In spite of Potemkin's protection, Sarti fell out of favor shortly afterwards.

In December 1787, Sarti was joined in St. Petersburg by Domenico Cimarosa (1749–1801), and shortly afterwards by the Spanish composer Vicente Martin y Soler (1754–1806)—his *Una cosa rara* is also quoted in the dinner scene of *Don Giovanni*—who was given the new title of Kappellmeister to the Russian court. Cimarosa remained in Russia until 1791. By then, Catherine the Great had considerably reduced the size of the Italian opera company. Sarti, after a brief period spent in the Ukraine, returned to favor in 1793 and became director of St. Petersburg's first music conservatory. He left Russia after the death of Paul I and died in Berlin on the way home.

ENEA NEL LAZIO

Opera in due Atti con balli analoghi

da rappresentarsi

Nell' Imperial Teatro di Gatchina

in occasione delle faustissime nozze

di Sua Altezza Imperiale

La Gran Duchessa

ELENA PAVLOVNA

con Sua Altezza Serenissima

FEDERICO LUIGI

Principe Ereditario

di Mecklenbourg - Schwerin.

San Pietroburgo nella Stamperia Imperiale
MDCCXCIX.

Personaggi.

Latino, Re del Lazio.
  Sigr. *Paolo Mandini.*

Lavinia, sua figlia.
  Siga. *Maciorletti.*

Enea, Principe Trojano.
  Sigr. *Testori.*

Turno, Re dei Rutoli.
  Sigr. *Cristofori.*

Coro { Di Soldati Trojani.
      { Di Popoli del Lazio.

La musica del Sigr. *Giuseppe Sarti*, Consigliere di Collegio, e Maestro di Cappella al Servizio di S. M. I.

Le Decorazioni sono del Sigr. *Gonsaga.*

Plany feiverka po vysochaishemu poveleniiu dannago v Sankt-Peterburgie na ploshchadi protiv Tavricheskago Dvortsa 7go Genvaria 1809go goda (Plan of the fireworks given by His Imperial Majesty in St. Petersburg on the square facing the Tauride Palace on 7 January 1809). Original pen-and-ink and wash drawing. [St. Petersburg, 1809?]

The Tauride Palace, the site of the elaborate display of fireworks illustrated in this album of three drawings, was built by the Muscovite architect Ivan Starov (1744–1808) on land given to Catherine's favorite, Prince Grigorii Aleksandrovich Potemkin (1739–91). It was erected in 1783–88 while Potemkin was on the Black Sea, and presented to him as a gift on his return in 1789. One year later, Catherine agreed to buy it from him to let him pay his debts but she gave it to him again in 1790, when he was named Prince of Tauris to commemorate his conquest of Crimea (or Tauris in ancient Greek). Following Potemkin's death in 1791, Catherine bought the palace back from his heirs. It is built in the austere neo-Palladian style favored by the empress, and famous in particular for its Colonnade Hall (then the largest such hall in Europe), its winter garden, designed by the British landscape architect William Gould, and the English garden on its grounds. A spectacular feast was hosted by Potemkin for Catherine at the Tauride Palace on 28 April 1791 to celebrate the capture of the city of Ismail by the Russian troops.

The fireworks depicted in the album were part of the celebration of the wedding of Grand-Duchess Ekaterina Pavlovna, the sister of Tsar Alexander I, and the Grand Duke of Oldenburg, in the presence of the King and Queen of Prussia. Napoleon had hoped to obtain Ekaterina's hand following the Tilsit interview and was subsequently denied that of her younger sister Anne (the future queen of Holland). His invasion of the Grand-Duchy of Oldenburg was one of the causes of the resumption of hostilities between France and Russia in 1812.

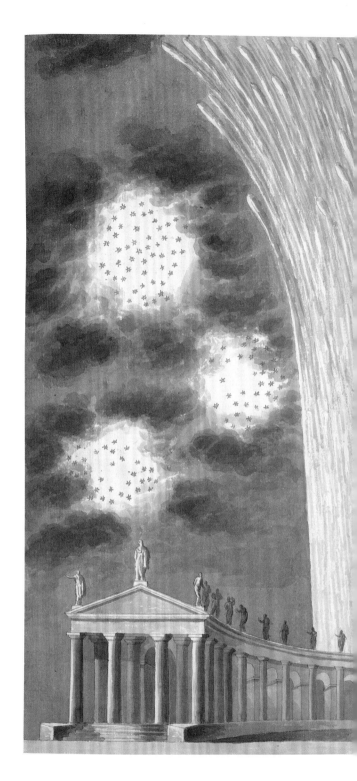

Luigi Rusca. *Recueil des dessins de différens batimens construits à Saint-Pétersbourg et dans l'intérieur de l'Empire de Russie / Raccolta dei disegni di diverse fabbriche costruite in Pietroburgo, e nell' interno dell' impero russo.* [St. Petersburg, 1810]. Paul Mellon Collection, Yale Center for British Art; Arts of the Book Collection, Sterling Memorial Library.

The Swiss architect Luigi Rusca (1758–1822) was a disciple and assistant of Quarenghi. He remained court architect in St. Petersburg until 1818. As shown by the record of his architectural drawings, engraved in Paris and published in St. Petersburg with a dedication to Alexander I, he was involved in a variety of civil and military projects, such as the barracks and headquarters of the Horseguards along the Neva, the post-1801 restoration and completion of the Tauride Palace, which went through a period of neglect under the reign of Paul I, and the addition of a gallery on the Admiralty side of the Winter Palace and the neighboring embankment.

The Arts of the Book copy of Rusca's *Recueil* comes from the Imperial Library at Tsarskoe Selo, which was largely dispersed after the Revolution. The views and perspectives (as opposed to plans) are hand-colored.

Luigi Rusca, arch.   *Gravé par J. E. Thierry.*

Vue perspective de la promenade de l'amir.té, du coté de la Néva et du Palais Impérial.

"Actes relatifs à la nouvelle organisation de la bibliothèque impériale. Traduits du russe par Marie-Félicité Brosset."
Manuscript [1841]

The oldest library of St. Petersburg is that of the Academy of Sciences, originating from Peter the Great's personal collection, which was already accessible to the public in his lifetime. It numbered 36,000 volumes by the end of the eighteenth century. Various other institutions, such as the Cadets Corps and the Academy of Fine Arts, had their own libraries. The idea of a truly public state library is to be credited to Count Aleksandr Stroganov (1738–1811) who, as early as 1766, issued a plan for an Imperial Public Library. This plan was embraced by Catherine the Great, who supervised the planning of the building designed by Igor Sokolov on Nevsky Prospect and erected in 1796–1801, between the space now occupied by the Alexandra Theater and Vallin de la Mothe's famous merchant galleries (Gostinyi Dvor) built between 1761 and 1785. The library building was later expanded by the Venetian Carlo Rossi (1775–1849), the leading Petersburg architect of the Romantic period.

While the founding of what is now the Russian National Library took place in 1795, it was opened to the public only on 2/14 January 1814, under Alexander I. The decrees and regulations copied and translated in this manuscript, presumably from originals in the library's archives, are the first in Russian history dealing with the state library.

The documents are as follows: Alexander I's instructions to Stroganov, dated 14 October 1810, concerning the library's forthcoming opening to the public; the statutes of the new library, also dated 14 October 1810 (article 16 gives it the status of copyright library on the same level as the library of the Academy of Sciences, while article 18 provides for its right to obtain copies of any manuscripts of historical signifance); the organizational chart of the library (including the salaries of its employees); decrees of 1811–12 following the death of Count Stroganov; and the detailed set of rules, dated 23 February 1812, governing the administration of the library. The rules, signed at the end by Count Alexis Razumovsky, comprise 95 articles, organized in three sections: 1) Responsibilities of the employees of the Imperial Public Library; 2) Rules to observe concerning library buildings; 3) Of the people visiting the library (opening hours and procedures, with a special section devoted to the manuscripts department, and a final section encouraging gifts to the library).

The compiler of this translation, identified on the spine of the slipcase as well as by a note pencilled on the first page, is the distinguished orientalist Marie-Félicité Brosset (1802–80), also known as Xavier or, during his years in Russia, Marie Ivanovich. Trained in Arabic and Chinese, he specialized in the Georgian and Armenian languages, then ignored by the École des langues orientales in Paris, and published extensively on those subjects. Having failed to get a position at that school, he became a printer at the Imprimerie nationale in 1835. In April 1837, thanks to the support of Russian friends, he was officially appointed a member of the Imperial Academy of Sciences in St. Petersburg, where he taught oriental languages and pursued his research. During the many years he spent in Russia, he participated in scientific missions to collect oriental manuscripts and study ancient civilizations. He occupied various official functions in St. Petersburg, including secretary and vice-president of the Academy of Sciences, and curator of medals at the Hermitage Museum. He returned to France in 1880 and died in Châtellerault in September of that year.

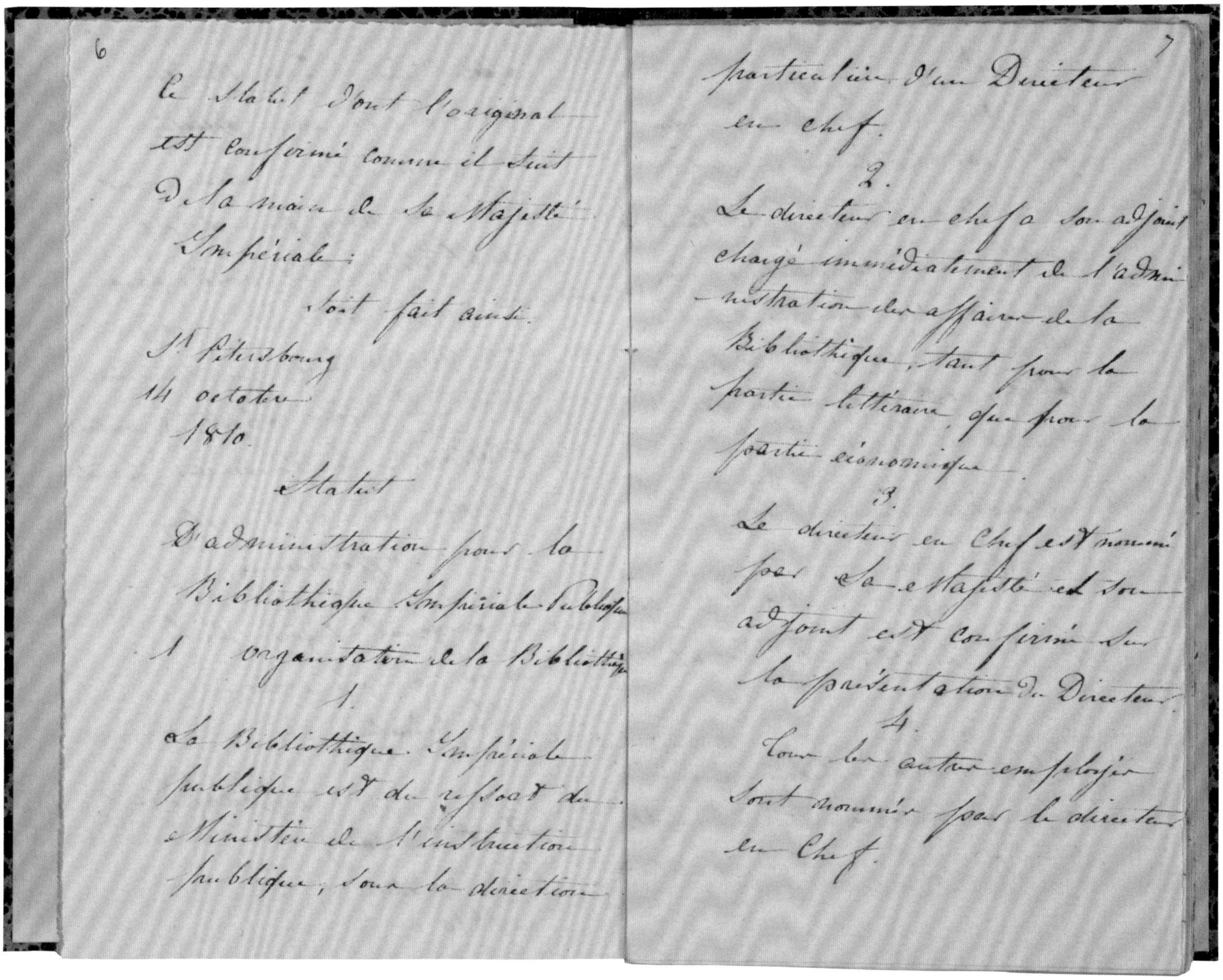

le Statut dont l'original
est conformé comme il suit
de la main de Sa Majesté
Impériale;

Soit fait ainsi.

St. Petersbourg
14 octobre
1810.

Statut

D'administration pour la
Bibliothèque Impériale publique

1. organisation de la Bibliothèque

1.

La Bibliothèque Impériale
publique est du ressort du
Ministre de l'instruction
publique, sous la direction

particulier d'un Directeur
en chef.

2.

Le directeur en chef a son adjoint
chargé immédiatement de l'administration des affaires de la
Bibliothèque, tant pour la
partie littéraire, que pour la
partie économique.

3.

Le directeur en chef est nommé
par Sa Majesté et son
adjoint est confirmé sur
la présentation du Directeur.

4.

Tous les autres employés
sont nommés par le directeur
en chef.

II. Visits to St. Petersburg in the Romantic Period

Kotzebue.

From an original Drawing
by Bolt of Berlin.

London, Printed for R. Phillips, N.º 71, St Paul's Church Y.º Feb.10.1802.

THE

MOST REMARKABLE YEAR

IN

THE LIFE

OF

AUGUSTUS VON KOTZEBUE;

CONTAINING AN ACCOUNT OF

HIS EXILE INTO SIBERIA,

AND OF

The other extraordinary Events which happened to him

IN RUSSIA.

WRITTEN BY HIMSELF.

TRANSLATED FROM THE GERMAN, BY

THE REV. BENJAMIN BERESFORD,

English Lecturer to the Queen of Prussia.

IN THREE VOLUMES.

VOL. I.

London:
PRINTED FOR RICHARD PHILLIPS,
No. 71, St. Paul's Church-yard.
By T. Gillet, Salisbury-square.

1802.

The Mikhailovsky (or Engineers') Castle,
by Sadovnikov (ca. 1833).

August von Kotzebue. *The most remarkable year in the life of Augustus von Kotzebue; containing an account of his exile into Siberia, and of the other extraordinary events which happened to him in Russia. Translated from the German, by the Rev. Benjamin Beresford, English lecturer to the Queen of Prussia.* London: Richard Phillips, 1802.

The prolific Weimar-born playwright had been appointed by Catherine the Great counsellor to the Duchy of Estonia in 1783 and, two years later, at the age of 24, chief justice and president of the government of the province. Catherine II continued to extend her protection to Kotzebue when he ran into difficulties over his satirical play *Doktor Bahrdt mit der eisernen Stirn* (1790). He resigned his position in Estonia but, after an unsuccessful tenure as manager of the Imperial Theater in Vienna and a short stay in Weimar, decided to return to Russia in the spring of 1800. After crossing the border, he was arrested by the police of Paul I on suspicions of having revolutionary sympathies and sent to Siberia, where he was held for four months, before being unexpectedly pardoned and compensated by the tsar with the gift of an estate and the appointment as director of the German Theater in St. Petersburg. This remarkable story forms the substance of the memoir *Das merkwürdigste Jahr meines Lebens*, published in 1801 and translated into English the following year. Kotzebue had by then left Russia for good, although he was made a councellor of state by Alexander I in 1816. Suspicions that he was a Russian intelligence agent eventually led to his assassination in 1819 at his home in Mannheim by the student Karl Ludwig Sand.

Nearly half of Kotzebue's memoir takes place in St. Petersburg. He evokes his first interview with Paul I, who immediately set him to translate into French a bizarre challenge to the sovereigns of Europe to settle their quarrels in a kind of public tournament. A more rational commission followed, that of preparing, with Sarti's help, a French version of Haydn's *Creation*, to be performed at the Hermitage Theater. The tsar next recruited Kotzebue to write a description of the recently completed Mikhailovsky Castle, built for him, and according to his instructions, by Vasilii Bazhenov and Vincenzo Brenna. An abbreviated version of Kotzebue's description occupies a substantial part of the third volume. At the end is an account of his last meeting with Paul I on 11 March 1801, a few hours before the tsar's assassination in his new residence, which had been planned especially to protect him against such a fate, and where he had

The Beinecke library of th William Beck had his penc found at the beginning of the third volume and have to do with Kotzebue's description of the Mikhailovsky Castle. He evidently took exception to phrases such as "an abortive son of the Muses and Graces" (applied by Kotzebue to a painter whose name is given as Smuglevitsch), "allegorical bas-reliefs, that set all explanation at defiance" ("N.B.," comments Beckford, "These sorts of production are not confined to the palace of Michaïloff"), "an allegorical ceiling . . . very difficult to unravel." "By this time," Beckford comments, "I should hope, these confounded allegories have ceased to puzzle inquisite travellers. The palace scarcely finished was smouldering by piecemeal tho' warmed by 1000 fires in stoves & chimneys—Having been left cold & desolate since the Emp'r's murder there can be no doubt of its destruction.—a few weeks after Paul's death it began to look like a Mausoleum." As Beckford never set foot in Russia, his information may have come from his son-in-law, the 10th Duke of Hamilton, who was British ambassador in St. Petersburg from 1806 to 1808.

In 1823, the Mikhailovsky Castle was acquired by the Guards Corps of Engineers and it has been known since as the Engineers' Castle, to distinguish it from the new Mikhailovsky Palace, built in 1819–25 by Rossi for Grand Duke Mikhail Pavlovich, brother of Alexander I and Nicholas I; since 1898, it has been the home of the Russian Museum.

Sir Robert Ker Porter. *Travelling sketches in Russia and Sweden during the years 1805, 1806, 1807, 1808. Second edition.* London: John Stockdale, 1813.

The Durham-born Ker Porter (1777–1842) was a student of Benjamin West. He became famous in 1800 for his panoramic painting of *The storming of Seringapatam*, exhibited at the Lyceum, after which he produced more such sensational battle scenes (Lodi, Alexandria, Acre etc.). In 1804, he was appointed historical painter to the Russian court and worked on the Admiralty Hall. It appears that he had to leave St. Petersburg precipitously after an incipient affair with Prince Shcherbatov's daughter, whom he eventually married after he returned to Russia in 1811. He subsequently published a *Narrative of the campaign of Russia during the year 1812,* was knighted by the Prince Regent, and resumed his journeys, which resulted in his massive *Travels in Georgia, Persia, Armenia, Ancient Babylonia, 1817–1820*, published in four volumes in 1821. He died in St. Petersburg as he was preparing to return to England and is buried in the English capital. His sister was the celebrated novelist Jane Porter (1776–1850).

Ker Porter's account of Russia was first published in London in 1809 and issued in Philadelphia in the same year. It is abundantly illustrated by his own drawings, even though he claims that many more were accidentally destroyed during his return trip. The book proper takes the form of letters to an unidentified friend. The first sixteen are dated from St. Petersburg between September 1805 and February 1806. However, the first letter, though written in Russia, deals entirely with Denmark and *Hamlet,* and the second with getting from Kronshtadt to the city. The third letter eloquently conveys the impression made by the size and splendor of the town: "Every house seems a palace, and every palace a city."

The statue of Peter the Great is discussed in Letter IV and generally much admired. The description, however, gives a somewhat strange account of Marie-Anne Collot's contribution to the statue by suggesting an infatuation, not with Falconet, but with Peter the Great: "She loved his person and adored his mind. The wonderful bust which she modelled of him, declares what a godlike image of himself he had stamped on her heart; and the divine manner with which she has given this impression to the eyes of men, is beyond description perfect. Falconet saw this bust, and from its breathing lines formed the head of his statue." Ker Porter is particularly enthusiastic about the horse, declaring it superior to the ones from San Marco (which he saw in Paris, where Napoleon, after having them removed from Venice, installed them on the triumphal arch at the Carrousel).

The following letter describes the usual sites: the Summer Garden, the Red Palace (as Paul I's Mikhailovsky Castle was known), the Winter Palace, the Hermitage. Letter VI discusses the Academy of Fine Arts and the Tauride Palace (with due acknowledgment of William Gould, "the Repton of Russia"). The next four letters are devoted to the Alexander Nevsky Monastery and the Russian Orthodox Church, with long quotations from the main rituals. Letter XI, dated October 1805, begins with a description of the frozen Neva, sledges, and sledge-races: "The surrounding winter scenery; the picturesque sledges and their fine horses; the scattered groups of the observing multitude; the superb dresses of the nobility, their fur cloaks, caps, and equipages, adorned with coloured velvets and gold, finish the scene, and make it seem like an Olympic game from the glowing pencil of Rembrandt."

Letter XII contains sketches of Generals Kutuzov and Bagration, while letter XIII relates a visit to Tsarina Elizabeth, leading to a comparison between Elizabeth I of England and Catherine the Great ("What Elizabeth was to England, Catherine the Second was to Russia"). The letter is dramatically interrupted by the news of the victory of Trafalgar and the death of Lord Nelson, and ends with patriotic meditations on the eve of the battle of Austerlitz, the news of which is reported in Letter XIV, while the next letter describes Alexander I on his return. Letter XVI, in keeping with the climate of the hour, is entirely devoted to a description of the Russian army.

The Beinecke copy of the second edition of Ker Porter's *Travelling sketches* comes from the famous library of Comte Riant, acquired jointly by Harvard and by Yale at the end of the nineteenth century—Yale's acquisition being made possible by a gift from the widow of Henry Farnam, the railroad magnate whose house on Hillhouse Avenue is now the President's House.

Damaze de Raymond. *Tableau historique, géographique, militaire et moral de l'empire de Russie.* Paris: Le Normant, 1812.

This survey of Russia was published in the year when Napoleon invaded the country. About the author, Damaze de Raymond (1770–1813), little more is known than what appears on the title page: a trained diplomat, he was, as of 1802, a chargé d'affaires to the Republic of Ragusa (i.e., Dalmatia, Ragusa being the Italian name of Dubrovnik), a member of the electoral college of the département of Lot-et-Garonne (the Toulouse area), and a member of the agricultural, scientific, and artistic society of Agen. He must have sojourned in Russia before 1811 but in what capacity is not known. The *Dictionary of French Biography* indicates that he was then employed by the *Journal de l'Empire*, essentially a mouthpiece for the regime, where he contributed, according to the author of the *D.F.B.* entry, ill-informed polemical articles, supposedly to detract attention from the bad news on all military fronts. The same source casts doubts on Damaze de Raymond's morality and reports that he was killed in a duel following a quarrel in a gambling house.

The first volume contains a historical précis from the origins until the death of Paul I, followed by a geographical and economic survey. The first section of the second volume is devoted to the population of Russia, the second section to St. Petersburg, the third chiefly to Moscow, and the fourth and last to other parts of the Russian empire.

The map of St. Petersburg bound in the second volume clearly predates the book by several years since the Admiralty is still represented surrounded by a moat and fortifications, which were removed in 1806. It shows the development of the city after its first hundred years and indicates particularly clearly its division into ten districts. It also reveals that the development of Vasilievsky Island was still limited. The list of monuments comprises almost entirely official and religious buildings.

Damaze de Raymond's somewhat flippant and not always well-informed account of the city is preceded by derogatory general considerations ("Petersburg is not the city of the Russians, it is the city of foreign artists paid by Russia"). Yet, the description proper is sympathetic and abounds in superlatives: "dazzling and magical tableau," "shore of the most delightful aspect," "magnificent" (twice in a page), "magical effect." "All is young, fresh, new in this town." The Winter Palace, on the other hand, is deemed in bad taste (the architect's name, possibly as a printer's error, is given as Rostretti), as is the Peter and Paul Cathedral. The newly completed Kazan Cathedral gets high marks and the Alexander Nevsky Monastery the highest of all. Chapter 10 is devoted to arts and sciences and mentions "Lomonoskof" [i.e., M. V. Lomonosov] and "the famous Sumorokof, father of the theater" [i.e, A. P. Sumarokov]. The brief description of the imperial residences, in chapter 14, is mixed: the gardens of Peterhof are no match for Versailles; those of Tsarskoe Selo are praised, but its "heavy and detestable" architecture is not (the Alexander Palace is much preferred); Pavlovsk and Gatchina get honorable mentions.

Plan de St. Petersbourg

Gotthilf Theodor von Faber. *Bagatelles. Promenades d'un désoeuvré dans la ville de S.-Pétersbourg.* Paris: Klostermann; Delaunay, 1812.

This delightful, familiar account of St. Petersburg, also dated from the year of Napoleon's invasion of Russia, is a first-hand description of everyday life in the Russian capital by someone who lived, or at least spent some time there, and had personal contacts with the inhabitants. There is evidence that he stayed there long enough to learn the language and get invited to clubs ("Château-Margaux is served as house wine"); and several chapters contain sympathetic vignettes of his Russian servant Fedor, whose propensity to drunkenness is easily forgiven.

About the anonymous author, not much is known apart from his dates (1766–1847). His self-description as a "désoeuvré" (which literally implies unemployed, but may simply mean dilettante) is not explained in the text. Faber also published *Notices sur l'intérieur de la France, écrites en 1806*; these appeared in London (two editions in 1811 and 1813) and Philadelphia (1812), and in German translation in 1815. According to the *British Museum Catalogue*, he also supplied a preface to *Bemerkungen über die französische Armee der neuesten Zeit*, published in 1808. Faber was clearly German-born, but there is no indication that this book is a translation, nor is there evidence of a German edition. There are a few references to Germany, but the many more to Paris and the French (as well as his 1806 *Notices*) seem to indicate that the author lived mostly in France and wrote his account of St. Petersburg with a French readership in mind. Thus, chapter 9 of the first volume, "La ressemblance," is a parallel between the Russians and the French ("The Russians have inexhaustible reserves of gaiety; they are the French of the North"), and the chapter on Gostinyi Dvor, entitled "Le Palais-royal," consists of a comparison between the two merchant galleries of Paris and Petersburg.

As the title promises, the book is not organized in a systematic fashion. The first chapter, "Devinez où vous êtes?" (Guess where you are), imagines that one could be magically transported to various parts of St. Petersburg and, blindfolded, asked to guess where one is; this charming passage was quoted in English translation in Svin'in's *Sketches of Russia* (1814) and the first part of his *Description of St. Petersburg* (1816).

The second chapter, "L'aplomb," gives examples of the apparent natural courage of Russians in everyday life. The following chapters have lively titles such as "Les traversées" (Crossings), "L'homme indépendant," "La nuit et le jour" (on White Nights), "Le piéton" (Pedestrians), "Voir et être vu" etc.

As the title and subtitle also indicate, the book has no ambition except to be a lively personal account of the city. It thus contains no historical survey or political considerations (except perhaps to deplore, in the final chapter of the second volume, the lack of a serious, independent newspaper). Even the description of the architecture of the city is mostly a record of personal impressions (some, such as the phrase "On peut appeler la ville aux St. Petersburg la ville aux colonnes," were later borrowed by other writers). Yet the book is not devoid of serious considerations. The second volume opens with a chapter ("Ne condamnez pas") praising the religious tolerance in vigor in St. Petersburg. Chapter 7 of the second volume ("Les malheureuses") deals with prostitutes in St. Petersburg. After general considerations on prostitution ("there ought to be a kind of right of women, which men should respect"), the author deplores the bad public treatment of prostitutes he has witnessed in the Russian capital.

BAGATELLES.

Jean-Baptiste Joseph Breton. *La Russie, ou moeurs, usages, et costumes des habitants de toutes les provinces de cet empire. Ouvrage orné de cent-onze planches, représentant plus de deux cents sujets, gravés sur les dessins originaux et d'après nature, de M. Damame-Démartrait [sic], peintre français, auteur et éditeur des Maisons de Plaisance impériales de Russie, et Robert Ker-Porter, peintre anglais, inventeur des panoramas.* Paris: Nepveu, 1813.

"This work was not inspired by the current circumstances," writes the author to open his preface. Despite this disclaimer, there was considerable interest in Russia and Russian things in 1813 in France, following Napoleon's retreat from Moscow. The preface also claims that the work has no scientific pretensions and is intended for a worldly readership of both sexes. It is, in fact, a compilation drawn from various sources. As the preface acknowledges, the work is heavily indebted to Ker Porter's *Travelling sketches*. Breton also acknowledges that certain parts of his work are borrowed from Edward Daniel Clarke's *Travels in various countries of Europe, Asia and Africa*, the London publication of which began in 1810. Another source turns out to be Faber (an "ingenious writer"), whose *Bagatelles* are quoted in the description of St. Petersburg. A more obscure one is Dietrich Wilhelm Soltau's *Briefe über Russland und dessen Bewohner* (Berlin, 1811).

The Russian capital occupies chapters 4 to 11, the last three being in the second volume.

The statue of Peter the Great is described in some detail, mostly after Ker Porter, whom he misreads on the subject of Collot, suggesting that she was romantically involved with Peter the Great (Breton apparently not being aware that she was born 23 years after the tsar's death), with additional references to Fortia de Piles's *Voyage de deux Français en Allemagne*, published in 1796. Breton also quotes "the scientist Pallas" predicting that within two or three centuries the surface of the statue's rocky pedestal "will be completely deteriorated and show a hideous aspect, if it has not fallen altogether into dust."

The compiler, known as Breton de La Martinière (1777–1852), began his career as stenographer to the National Assembly during the French Revolution. During Napoleon's reign, he produced a series of travel books (all presumably "drawn from the best authors," to borrow Stendhal's immortal phrase) on Belgium, Piedmont, Spain and Portugal, Egypt and Syria, China, and Japan. After the Bourbon Restoration, he saluted the régime change with a pamphlet and resumed his functions as stenographer to the Assembly. He was one of the founders of the *Gazette des tribunaux* in 1825. While discussing the Hermitage, he mentions in a footnote that he owns a precious stone, engraved in the ancient manner, that Catherine the Great had presented to Diderot.

The views of the Stone Theater and of St. Isaac Square are copied from Ker Porter, as are most of the costume plates, which constitute the majority of the illustrations. Other illustrations are by Michel-François Damame-Demartrais (1763–1827), a pupil of David, who moved to Russia in 1796. In 1806, he published a series of plates of Russian carriages, and is also known for *Une année de S.-Pétersbourg, ou douze vues pittoresques de cette capitale*, an album of 36 plates showing Russian imperial residences and their gardens, published in 1811, and smaller series of views of the main cities of Russia (1813). The folding plate showing carnival scenes in St. Petersburg is attributed to a mysterious Guasenchi—evidently a misprint for Quarenghi.

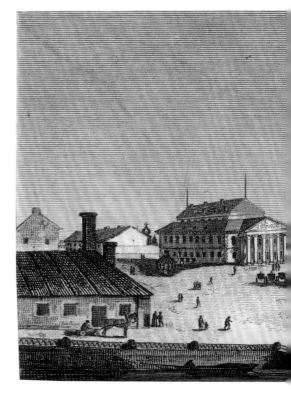

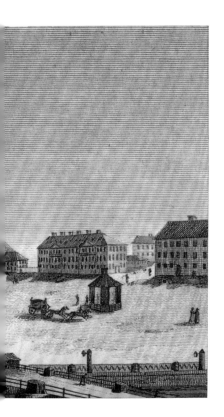

Federigo Fagnani. *Lettere scritte di Pietroburgo correndo gli anni 1810 e 1811.* Milan: Giovanni Bernardoni, 1815.

The Marchese Fagnani published a first series of "Letters written from St. Petersburg" in Milan in 1812. According to the title page of the 166-page volume, they cover the years 1811–12; Fagnani then bore the title of count, which he has kept in library catalogues. This much longer series for the years 1810–11, in two volumes, was issued three years later, also in Milan, but by a different publisher. In spite of the different years in the title, it is a reprint of the first series (the six letters in question are signalled by an asterisk in the table), with fourteen additional letters.

The folding map bound at the end of the first volume superficially resembles the one found in Damaze de Raymond's contemporary *Tableau*, but is in fact posterior. It also contains many more numbered references, including numbers for the streets of the city, even though Fagnani stops short of listing these in the accompanying table.

The undated letters (save for a reference to arriving in Stockholm in early October 1810) are written, like those of Ker Porter, to an unidentified, and therefore possibly fictitious, correspondent. That this might be the case is suggested by their strict thematic arrangement, laid out in the opening table ("Argomenti delle lettere"). The first deals, as usual, with the journey and arrival, and the second gives a general idea of the city and its chief monuments and sites (with a reference to Fortia de Piles, whose work is mentioned more than once throughout the letters). Fagnani then describes the Academy of Fine Arts, adding considerations on the general state of the arts in Russia. The fourth letter is mostly devoted to the statue of Peter the Great, with an interesting comparison of the rock with Bernini's fountain on the Piazza Navona. In the fifth letter, one of the longest, the author then discusses the present state of architecture in St. Petersburg. An admirer of the "immortal Palladio," Fagnani praises the new Kazan Cathedral, which he describes in detail at the beginning of the sixth letter; this also contains a glowing account of the Hermitage Palace ("questo palazzo magico") and its Palladian theater.

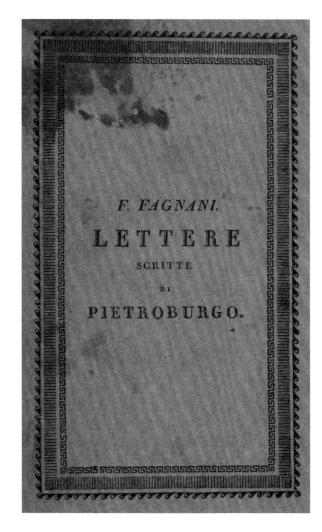

The seventh letter is devoted to "Precautions one takes in Russia to protect oneself against the cold," the eighth to Russian (i.e. steam) baths, always a subject of fascination to foreign visitors since Chappe d'Auteroche's 1768 account of Russia (not to mention Ibrāhīm Ibn Jaqūb's in the tenth century). The description is illustrated in a series of engravings at the end of the volume. The ninth letter deals with theater and conversation, while the brief tenth letter, which concludes the first volume, describes "Russian mountains" (another common subject of puzzled interest to visitors).

The second volume opens with considerations "on the rapid progress of the Russian people towards civilization." The next three letters deal with hospitals and charity, the fourth and fifth with education, the seventh with the army, the eighth with the Mint and the Imperial Bank. The penultimate letter is in the form of an essay on political relations in Russia. It is the only one that contains notes, which constitute a lengthy appendix to the second volume. The last one mentions food and drink and various aspects of everyday life and is followed by a brief conclusion.

The Lombard nobleman was a famous art and book collector. His collection, given to the Biblioteca Ambrosiana at his death, is reportedly the largest bequest ever received by that institution.

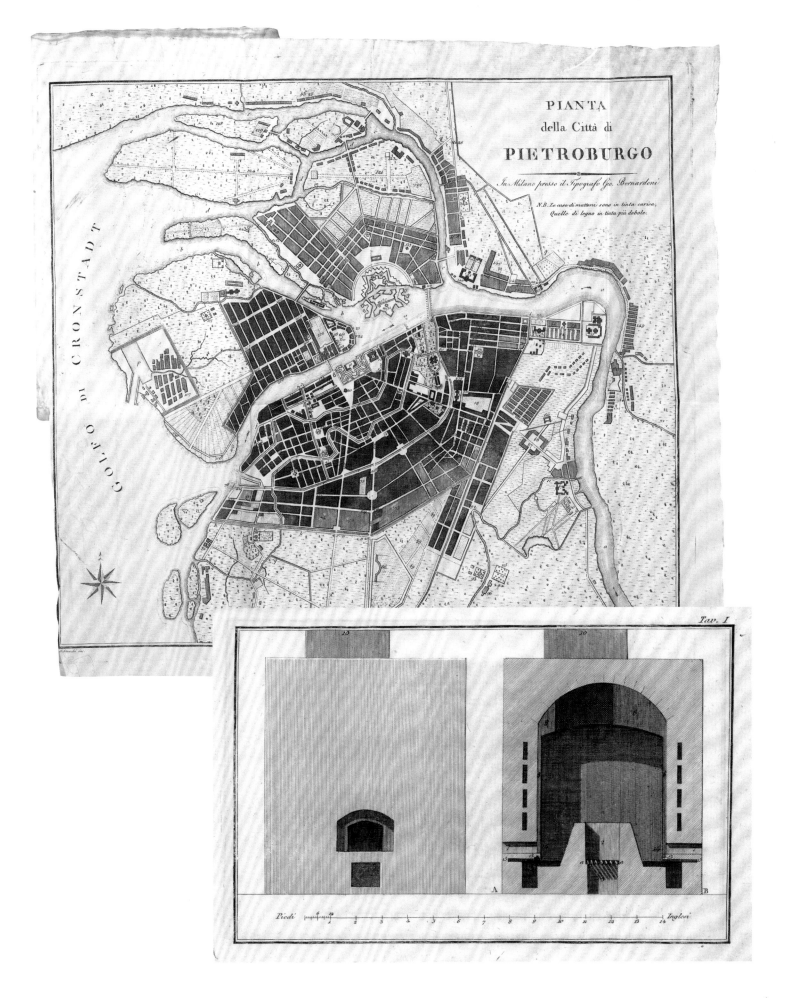

Robert Johnston. *Travels through part of the Russian empire and the country of Poland; along the southern shores of the Baltic.* London: J.J. Stockdale, 1815.

Unknown to biographical sources, Robert Johnston has left no other publication than this account of a trip he undertook between July and October 1814, according to the dates at the head of the chapters. It appeared with a dedication to the Prince Regent and was reprinted in New York in 1816.

The book is illustrated with two engraved maps, published by Stockdale, and twenty colored plates by six different engravers (C.J. Canton, T. Cartwright, H. Dawe, J. Gleadah, J. Hill, and C. Williams) after Johnston's own drawings.

The account is organized in twelve chapters, only the third and fourth of which are devoted to St. Petersburg. Johnston's narrative is little more than a travel diary, even though it is shy of personal explanations (the "we" of his travelling party is never explicated). Steam baths ("no sight can be more disgusting that that exhibited in those places") and Russian mountains (called "flying mountains") do not fail to excite the curiosity of this rather stuffy tourist.

The Kazan Cathedral, one of his three views of St. Petersburg, was planned by Paul I as a rival to St. Peter's in Rome. He entrusted it to Brenna, the architect of his Red Palace, but the project was carried out by a team of Russian architects, sculptors, and painters. Consecrated in 1811, the church is mentioned by Johnston as not quite completed by the summer of 1814. Its peculiarity is due to the necessity to reconcile its location on the south side of Nevsky Prospect, with its northwest-southeast orientation, with the obligation for any Russian church to be turned towards the east. The cathedral built by Andrei Nikiforovich Voronikhin (a freed serf of Count Stroganov) is therefore not perpendicular, but parallel to the colonnade; another colonnade was originally planned on the south side, but never completed. As Johnston's crude, ill-proportioned rendering shows, Voronikhin designed a semi-circular place on the western side, surrounded by a sumptuous railing, at each end of which colossal statues of St. Peter and St. Paul were to be erected. The scheme was never realized and the railing, which Louis Réau reported to be badly deteriorated by 1913, no longer stands. On the other side lies the elegant Catherine Canal (now Griboedov), which Johnston makes to look almost like a sewer.

A picture of St. Petersburgh, represented in a collection of twenty interesting views of the city, the sledges, and the people. Taken on the spot at the twelve different months of the year: and accompanied with an historical and descriptive account. London: Edward Orme, 1815.

This description of St. Petersburg during the reign of Alexander I consists of an uncredited printed introduction and twenty plates: twelve views of various sites of the city, each for a different month (the January plate serves as frontispiece), and eight additional picturesque scenes showing sledges (in six cases) and carriages. The special engraved title page is in the shape of a crest with the arms of the Russian imperial family—the double-headed eagle, surmounted by the crown, and holding orb and scepter—, and a variant title: "A picture of St. Petersburgh. An Historical and Descriptive Account Accompanied with Twenty Plates of the Buildings, Carriages & People, from Drawings taken on the Spot, At the twelve different Months of the Year."

The twelve city plates are described as follows: "View of the imperial bank and shops" (January); "View of the Marble Palace in the Grande Millione" (February); "View of the Place and the Grand Theatre" (March); "View of the Parade and the Imperial Palace" (April); "View of the Place of Peter the Great, and the Senate House" (May); "View of the Neva, the Harbour, and the Exchange" (June); "View of the Canal of the Moika, the bridge, and the police establishment" (July); "View of the middle of the great bridge of the Neva, and of St. Petersburgh" (August); "View of the Champ de Mars, and the Summer Garden" (September); "View of the Place of Kasan, and the Cathedral" (October); "View of the Canal of the Fontanka, and the barracks" (November); "View of the Arsenal and the Foundry, in the Litanie" (December).

These color aquatints are the work of Clark and Dubourg after a certain Mornay, whose name does not appear to have been otherwise recorded. They are listed, with a brief commentary, in an "Explanation of the twelve plates, representing a year at S. Petersburgh," which appears twice in the volume, once in English, once in French. Similarly, the captions at the bottom of each plate are in the two languages, whereas the introduction is present only in English. This, of course, suggests that the plates themselves were produced with a continental, and possibly even the Russian market in mind.

A strong sense of the picturesque pervades the city views, which all feature a conspicuous human presence. Two of the buildings illustrated in the book were very recent at the time of publication: the Exchange, completed in 1809, flanked by the two rostral columns, the ensemble being the work of the Swiss-French architect Jean-François Thomas de Thomon, and the Kazan Cathedral, completed in 1811.

The 26-page introduction, entitled "The present state of St. Petersburgh," includes a brief historical survey, a few statistics, description of the main sites and monuments. The subject of sledges and transportation is covered at some length. The final four pages are more directly related to the plates, as they provide details on the life of the city throughout the year and on modes of transportation in winter. Though unsigned, it was chiefly compiled from Ker Porter's *Travelling sketches*, as many sections repeat his text verbatim.

A note on the verso of the first plate of the Beinecke copy indicates that it was purchased in Bath, in March 1825, by a certain John Goldsworthy.

Le Comte Joseph DE MAISTRE

LES SOIRÉES
DE
SAINT-PÉTERSBOURG,

OU

ENTRETIENS SUR LE GOUVERNEMENT TEMPOREL
DE LA PROVIDENCE :

SUIVIS

D'UN TRAITÉ SUR LES SACRIFICES;

PAR. M. LE COMTE JOSEPH DE MAISTRE,

ANCIEN MINISTRE DE S. M. LE ROI DE SARDAIGNE A LA COUR DE RUSSIE,
MINISTRE D'ÉTAT, RÉGENT DE LA GRANDE CHANCELLERIE, MEMBRE DE
L'ACADÉMIE ROYALE DES SCIENCES DE TURIN, CHEVALIER GRAND'CROIX
DE L'ORDRE RELIGIEUX ET MILITAIRE DE S. MAURICE ET DE S. LAZARE.

TOME PREMIER.

IMPRIMERIE DE COSSON.

PARIS,

LIBRAIRIE GRECQUE, LATINE ET FRANÇAISE,
RUE DE SEINE, N° 12.
M DCCC XXI.

Joseph de Maistre. *Les soirées de Saint-Pétersbourg, ou entretiens sur le gouvernement temporel de la Providence: suivis d'un traité sur les sacrifices.* Paris: Librairie grecque, latine et française, 1821.

"Nothing is rarer, nothing is more enchanting than a beautiful summer evening in St. Petersburg. Whether the length of the winter and the rarity of these nights, which gives them a particular charm, renders them more desirable, or whether they really are so, as I believe, they are softer and calmer than evenings in more pleasant climates. . . . The sun having descended below the horizon, the brilliant clouds shed a soft clarity, a golden half-light impossible to paint and that I have never seen elsewhere. The light and the shadows seem to mingle and conspire together to form a transparent veil covering the countryside. If heaven in its goodness reserved for me one of those moments so rare in life where the heart is flooded with joy by some extraordinary and unexpected happiness, if a wife, children, and brothers separated from me for a long time without hope of reunion were suddenly to tumble into my arms, I would want it to happen here. Yes, I would want it to be on one of those beautiful nights on the banks of the Neva among these hospitable Russians."

This striking, poetic description of White Nights opens Joseph de Maistre's *St. Petersburg Dialogues*, published a few months after his death in February 1821. As Jean-Louis Darcel's critical edition has revealed, it was, in fact, drafted by his younger brother Xavier, author of the once famous *Voyage autour de ma chambre*, and himself a resident of St. Petersburg from the time of his emigration in 1792 till his death in 1852.

Born in Chambéry (then part of the Kingdom of Savoy) in 1753, trained as a magistrate, Joseph de Maistre became a senator in 1788. Almost from the outset, he was a fierce opponent of the French Revolution. His anonymously published *Considérations sur la France* (1797), which proposed a providential interpretation of the events, was banned in that country and put him into trouble in his own. Having moved to Sardinia, he was appointed Sardinian ambassador in St. Petersburg, where he spent the years 1803–17, a prominent member of the émigré community as well as a secret adviser to Alexander I until he fell out of grace with the tsar and was recalled to Turin.

Maistre's book has been described by George Steiner as "together with Galileo's *Dialogo*, the most powerful philosophic-dramatic dialogues written in the West after Plato." It is in the form of eleven conversations—probably based on actual debates—among a royalist count (clearly standing for the author), a Russian senator (based on Vasilii Stepanovich Tamara, Russian ambassador to Constantinople), and a Bonapartiste French chevalier (probably modelled on François-Gabriel de Bray, Bavarian ambassador to Russia in 1809–12). The beauty of the setting (Maistre truly fell in love with the city of Peter the Great) contrasts sharply with the three men's discussion of the nature of evil, the importance of capital punishment, the significance of the suffering of innocents, and the necessity of monarchy.

Pavel Petrovich Svin'in. *Dostopamiatnosti Sanktpeterburga i ego okrestnostei. Description des objets les plus remarquables de St. Petersbourg et de ses environs.* St. Petersburg: V. Plavil'shchikov, 1816–28.

This bilingual publication, in Russian and French, was issued, according to the short preface, to rectify the lack of proper guides to the city, a lacuna compounded by the fact that most books on Russia have been written by foreign visitors and are therefore full of mistakes. It came out in five parts between 1816 and 1828. Given the absence of several prominent monuments (such as the Tauride Palace and Paul I's Mikhailovsky Castle), it is likely that more parts were intended.

The first section, published in 1816, begins with an overview of the capital (where Svin'in quotes the opening of Faber's *Bagatelles*) and a portrait (both in image and in words) of Alexander I. Next come descriptions of the Falconet statue, the Kazan Cathedral, the Summer Garden with its famous railing on the Neva side, carnival festivities, Pavlovsk, with a folding map of St. Petersburg in 1817 [sic]. The second part (1817), deals with the Alexander Nevsky Monastery, the Academy of Fine Arts, the Exchange, summer entertainments (swings), Tsarskoe Selo, and the Arsenal and Foundry. The third (1818) covers the Peter and Paul Fortress, Peter the Great's cabin, Strel'na, the hospice for the poor, fire and police services, and the Imperial Public Library (with a brief survey of the collections). The fourth part begins with a long section on the Hermitage and its collections (then including the libraries of Voltaire and Diderot, purchased by Catherine the Great) and also deals with Kronshtadt, the Semik festival (an annual celebration of spring held on the Sunday following the feast of the Ascension), and Rusca's 1818 Church of Our Lady of the Suffering. The fifth and last part (1828) describes the Stone Theater (with profiles of the main Russian actors of the current troupe and a brief survey of the history of the theater in Russia), the Navy Cadets Corps, the ceremony of the blessing of the waters on the feast of the Epiphany, the Admiralty, and Peterhof.

All sections, except for the one on Kronshtadt, are illustrated with a plate. Most of them are after Svin'in's own drawings (one is signed by Vorobieff). The engraver, Stepan Filippovich Galaktionov (1778–1854), who is in fact mentioned in the book in the section on the Academy of Fine Arts, was one of the foremost Russian printmakers of his day; he was also a book illustrator, most famously of Pushkin.

A diplomat and art collector as well as an accomplished artist, Svin'in (1788–1839) spent the years 1811–13 in the United States as secretary to the Russian Consul General, Andrei Dashkov. In 1813, he published, in Philadelphia, a volume entitled *Sketches of Russia and St. Petersburg*, issued the following year in London as *Sketches of Russia*, illustrated with fifteen engravings. The memoir Svin'in wrote on America, *Opyt zhyvopisnavo puteshestviia po severnoi Amerike* (An essay at a picturesque voyage in North America) was published in German translation in Riga in 1816; a Dutch translation appeared two years later, but it was only in 1930 that an English edition came out, in New York, illustrated with reproductions of his watercolors. He is also the author of a memoir of General Moreau, the French revolutionary commander who later joined the forces allied against Napoleon and was mortally wounded at the battle of Dresden in 1813. Svin'in met and befriended Moreau (then living in Morrisville, Pennsylvania) during his American stay. The memoir was first issued in French in 1814 and immediately published in English on both sides of the Atlantic. Other publications by Svin'in include *Ezhednevniia zapiski v Londonie* (Daily notes in London, St. Petersburg, 1817) and *Vospominaniia na flotie* (Reminiscences of the Navy, St. Petersburg, 1818). He was also the first editor of the magazine *Otechestvennyia zapiski* (Memoirs of the fatherland), published in St. Petersburg, serving in that capacity from 1818 until 1830.

In the 1820s, Svin'in, who belonged to the Imperial Academy of Fine Arts, founded the first St. Petersburg "Russian Museum," based on his own collections.

Svin'in's work, the first serious, comprehensive attempt at a description of St. Petersburg, is also notable in the way it anticipates the celebration of the city as a work of art by the writers and artists of the art periodical *Mir isskustva* eight decades later. Its evocative prose can be

Façade of the Imperial Public Library (now Russian National Library) and entrance to Gostinyi Dvor on Nevsky Prospect.

sampled in this description of the Summer Garden during White Nights:

"Come to this garden, during one of those beautiful nights in May or June, when one enjoys perpetual light. Sit down under that oak planted a hundred years ago, near the Fontanka, and while you breathe a pleasantly cool air, while around you is nothing but uninterrupted silence and your imagination is your sole company, you suddenly hear a sweet, voluptuous harmony; it slowly approaches and plunges all your senses into melancholy and the complete oblivion of all that surrounds us. Your imagination transports you beyond the frontiers of the world and you think you are hearing heavenly music . . . but suddenly a choir of ringing voices brings you out of your wonderment and you recognize Russian singers, slowly going down the silvery waters of the Neva in pretty barges. Enclosed in the confines of the garden, though in the middle of the city, you can breathe the pure air of the countryside while you contemplate in wonder the activity of the inhabitants of the city; you have before you the beauties of simple nature and the masterpieces of genius. Finally, take a few steps beyond the walls of the garden, you find yourself on the so-called Palace Embankment: there you see the Neva covered with merchant vessels; there the menacing fortress is reflected in the quiet mirror of its waters; further afield, the new Exchange offers itself to the view with its obelisks, like an ancient temple surrounded with magnificent edifices, while on the opposite side the eye agreeably dwells on flowery gardens and the pretty pleasure houses of the rich inhabitants of St. Petersburg. Those picturesque sights, at sunset, when the horizon is almost ablaze, form a coup d'oeil beyond description, one that you never tire of admiring."

Peter the Great's cabin.

The Stone Theater.

Illuminations at Peterhof.

Rusland, zijnde eene statistieke, aardrijks — en natuurkundige beschrijving van dat uitgebreide reik. Nieuwe uitgave. Amsterdam: J.C. van Kesteren, 1821.

This account of Russia was anonymously published in 1804 in Haarlem and reissued by a different publisher seventeen years later. The traditional attribution is to Pieter van Woensel, who had published in 1781 a survey of Russia which, as we have seen, focused mostly on St. Petersburg. But the book has also been credited to the more famous Johan (or Johannes) Meerman, lord of Vuren and Dalem (1753–1815), translator of Ovid, Molière, and Klopstock, and author of several travel books, especially *Eeenige berichten omtrent het Noorden en Noord-Oosten van Europa (1804–1806),* as well as a *Discours sur le premier voyage de Pierre le Grand, principalement en Hollande,* published in Paris in 1812.

Dedicated to J.H. van Kinsbergen, First Admiral of the Navy of the King of Denmark, *Rusland* is organized in eight books, preceded by an introduction. The first book contains mostly geographical and meteorological data. The second deals with the ethnic and religious backgrounds of the population of Russia. The third, by far the longest, divided into three subsections, is devoted to St. Petersburg; the fourth to the government; the fifth to the Russian army and navy; the sixth to finances; the seventh to industry and commerce. The final book, one of the briefest, is in the form of a conclusion on the political interests of Russia. A jocular appendix, entitled "pour la bonne bouche" and headed by three isolated exclamation marks, contains explanatory notes and acknowledgments.

At the beginning and end of each book are small picturesque woodcut vignettes of places and people; according to the appendix, these are the work of the Amsterdam painter Harmanus Fock (1766–1822). Fock also designed two folding plates, engraved by Jakob Ernst Marcus (1774–1826) and both dated 1804. Their subject is public amusements in winter and summer. The winter plate shows iced glissoires on the Neva, popular versions of the ones installed in the imperial residences of Oranienbaum and Tsarskoe Selo; in the background are the Academy of Sciences and Peter the Great's Kunstkammer. The summer plate shows an equally lively scene with the so-called "balançoires" (ancestors of our great Ferris wheels) and other kinds of slides.

As Svin'in explains in the chapter he devotes to these "balançoires," they were traditionally erected at Easter on St. Isaac Square and remained in place throughout the summer.

RUSLAND.

ZIJNDE

EENE STATISTIEKE, AARDRIJKS–EN NATUURKUNDIGE BESCHRIJVING

VAN

DAT UITGEBREIDE RIJK;

EENE BELANGRIJKE BIJDRAGE
TOT LAND–EN VOLKEREN–KENNIS.

Met gegraveerde Platen en Vignetten.

NIEUWE UITGAVE.

W.H.Hoogkamer del. et sculp.

Te AMSTERDAM, bij
J. C. VAN KESTEREN.
MDCCCXXI.

James Holman. *Travels through Russia, Siberia, Poland, Cracow, Austria, Bohemia, Saxony, Prussia, Hanover &c. &c. undertaken during the years 1822, 1823, 1824, while suffering from total blindness, comprising an account of the author being conducted a state prisoner from the eastern part of Siberia. Fourth edition.* London: Smith, Elder, and Co., 1834. Yale Center for British Art, Paul Mellon Fund.

One of the most unusual visitors to St. Petersburg in the Romantic period was James Holman (1786–1857), known as the blind traveller. A native of Exeter, he had been in the Royal Navy from 1798 until 1810. He served on the coasts of Britain and North America and reached the grade of lieutenant. Having lost his eyesight at the age of 25, he decided to go on his own on a series of travels abroad, which he subsequently published: the first through France and central Europe, in 1819–21; the second to Russia and Siberia in 1822–24; the third and most ambitious, around the world, including Africa, Brazil, various islands on the Indian Ocean, the Subcontinent, Singapore, China, Australia, and New Zealand. The fourth and final, through Spain and southern Europe, remained unpublished at his death. Holman was made a fellow of the Royal Society in 1825 and is described by the *Dictionary of National Biography* as "a man of remarkable energy and perseverance, of cool intrepidity and restless curiosity." That is the image conveyed by the frontispiece portrait by Wageman in his *Travels through Russia*, in which Holman is seen writing in a braille-like system, a painting of a ship in a stormy sea hanging behind him. In his preface, and at several points in the book, he justifies travel (or, as he puts it, locomotion) as a compensating principle, and explains how, by having to resort to all senses but vision, he strives to arrive at an "ideal" knowledge of places he visits. This quixotic enterprise, as the author himself qualifies it, seems to anticipate the writings of Ved Mehta in our own age. It did not spare him dismissive, patronizing comments by another traveller to Russia, Captain John Dundas Cochrane, whom he met in Moscow, and who, in 1824, published an account of his own exploration of Russia on foot.

Holman's account of his Russian trip was first issued in 1825 and went through three successive editions. Having left England on 19 June 1822 (the month is wrongly printed as July), he arrived at Kronshtadt on 10 July. Since he was travelling on his own, he immediately recruited an 18-year-old servant-cum-interpreter, while friends in the Petersburg English community provided him with introductions to Russians. He thus attended a particularly lively dinner party with Don Cossacks, which forms the subject of one of the illustrations, drawn according to his instructions. Holman remained in St. Petersburg until 13 March 1823. From there he went to Moscow and in June proceeded towards Siberia, reaching Irkutsk, where he spent the fall and Christmas, hoping to continue his exploration towards the Chinese border. On 2 January 1824, for reasons that he cannot explain, a Feldjäger was dispatched on imperial orders to bring him back to Moscow and, in effect, expel him from the country, which he left at the end of February, returning to England via Poland and Germany.

Chapters 4 to 12 of Holman's first volume are devoted to a general description of St. Petersburg: its palaces and chief monuments, manufactures, cultural and educational institutions (Holman admits his exposure to the theater was a strain), walks, sports and clubs, hotels and "eating-houses," social classes, religion, commerce, and winter pastimes. Chapter 8, devoted to the police, prisons, and firemen, describes their training: they climb on ladders to a four-story-high platform from which they have to jump, landing on a sail cloth held underneath by their colleagues, with additional protection of featherbeds, straw, or hay underneath. "I personally visited the scene of exercise," notes Holman, "accompanied by a friend, who obligingly made me a sketch of the apparatus employed, and which accompanies this description."

Gauci Jun.
Vol. 1 Page 123

Printed by Lefevre & Kohler 52 Newman Str.

Augustus Bozzi Granville. *St. Petersburgh. A journal of travels to and from that capital; through Flanders, the Rhenish Provinces, Prussia, Russia, Poland, Silesia, Saxony, the Federated States of Germany, and France.* London: Colburn, 1828.

The author, whose titles, enumerated on the title page, occupy twelve lines of small type, was born in 1783 in Milan, where his father was postmaster general (he was distantly related to the Bonaparte family). Granville, the name he later took at his mother's behest, was that of his maternal grandmother, whose own father had settled in Italy for political reasons. Granville studied medicine at the University of Pavia and gained employment as doctor to the Turkish fleet. He later was in Spain and Portugal, where he became surgeon to the English fleet stationed there. As of 1813 he was in London, where he lectured on chemistry while maintaining a keen interest in Italian political affairs. He then studied in Paris in 1816–17, becoming a distinguished obstetrician. After his seventeen-week trip to Russia in 1827, he published a highly successful *Catechism of Health* and became president of the Westminster Medical Society and vice-president of the British Medical Association. He visited St. Petersburg again in 1849, supplying Lord Palmerston, the prime minister, with details on the physical and mental health of Nicholas I. He died in 1872 at the age of 88 and his autobiography appeared two years later.

Granville, as he explains, went to St. Petersburg in July 1827 to accompany Count and Countess Mikhail Vorontsov. They reached the city on 27 October. Much of the first volume is actually occupied by an account of the journey, through Flanders, Saxony, and Prussia. The description of St. Petersburg occupies four chapters in the first volume and thirteen in the second, the remaining five being devoted to the return journey.

Granville begins with general considerations of the city, in which he bemoans the lack of printed guides and notes, by reference to his main source, Storch's 1801 description of the city, that "a more modern description of St. Petersburg than exists at present, is absolutely required" (the preface, in fact, suggests that his own book might be useful to travellers as a guide to the Russian capital). One interesting feature of Granville's book is that the map bound at the end of the first volume is divided into squares allowing one to find the location of the streets, sites, and monuments listed. The Bronze Horseman is described in detail and called "perhaps the finest— certainly the most correct statue of the kind in Europe." The next chapter is full of practical advice to travellers concerning transportation, registration, customs, accommodation, and the like. Granville then discusses climate, which leads him to a description of the Russian bath which, unlike his semi-compatriot Johnston, he describes as offering "the double advantage of promoting health and cleanliness." The fourth chapter deals chiefly with the Hermitage. There follows a particularly interesting portrait of Nicholas I as well as of other members of the imperial family, and a brief description of the government, leading naturally to the next three chapters, on public buildings and institutions. Granville pays particular attention to the state of science in Russia, which in this respect is "not on a level with that of other enlightened countries." Next come religion and churches, including a report on the progress of the colossal new cathedral of St. Isaac, on which the French architect Auguste Ricard de Montferrand worked from 1818 until his death in 1858, the year when the edifice was completed (Montferrand's request to be buried in his church was denied on religious grounds). Granville then surveys education and literature ("The name of Alexander Pouschkine, the Byron of Russia, is probably familiar to most English readers") before taking up his own subject of expertise, medicine, to which the entire chapter 11 is devoted.

Medicine in St. Petersburg, considered "en masse," is, according to Granville, "not so experimental as that of the German physicians; it is more expectant than that of the French; less bold and philosophical than that of the Northern Italians; and not quite so effectual and successful as that of the English." He lists the medical practitioners, Russian or foreign, he encountered during his visit and surveys the state of medical education in St. Petersburg.

The final chapters of Granville's memoir describe commerce, court ceremonies and public festivals and pastimes, music and sports, and street markets. Chapter 16 deals with the Russian legal system, Granville reporting at length on a conversation he had with a high-ranking St. Petersburg magistrate. The question of serfdom is broached with long quotations from another high-ranking official, chiefly in defense of the system. Chapter 17 includes descriptions of imperial residences around St. Petersburg and ends with the author's brief account of his presentation to Tsarina Alexandra.

Granville's book is illustrated throughout with unsigned illustrations, credited simply to his publisher, Henry Colburn.

Admiralty.   Bridge.   Labanoff.   Peter's Statue.   New Cathedral.

VIEW OF PART OF THE ADMIRALTY, THE PALAIS LABANOFF, THE PLACE AND BRIDGE ISAAC,
AND THE NEW CHURCH OF ST. ISAAC.

London : Published by Henry Colburn, August 1, 1828.

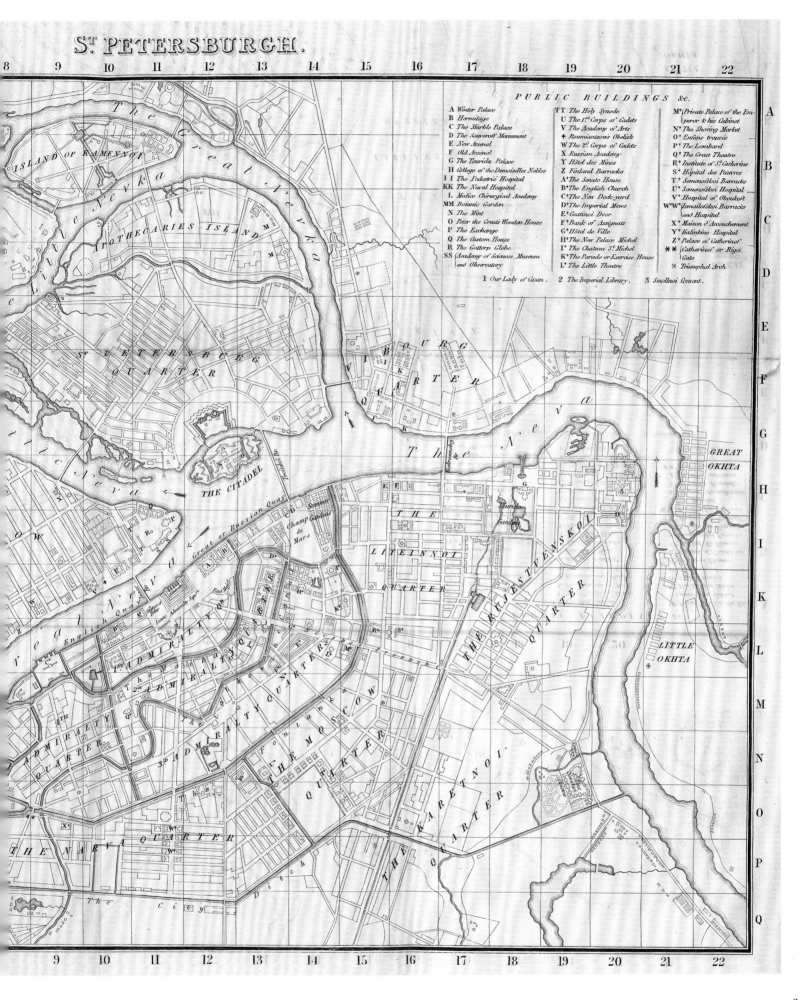

St. PETERSBURGH.

PUBLIC BUILDINGS &c.

A Winter Palace
B Hermitage
C The Marble Palace
D The Sotwaroff Monument
E New Arsenal
F Old Arsenal
G The Tourida Palace
H College of the Demoiselles Nobles
I I The Pedestrie Hospital
KK The Naval Hospital
L Medico Chirurgical Academy
MM Botanic Garden
N The Mint
O Peter the Greats Wooden House
P The Exchange
Q The Custom House
R The Gottorp Globe
SS Academy of Sciences Museum and Observatory

TT The Holy Synode
U The 1st Corps of Cadets
V The Academy of Arts
✦ Roumiantzow's Obelisk
W The 2d Corps of Cadets
X Russian Academy
Y Hôtel des Mines
Z Finland Barracks
A* The Senate House
B* The English Church
C* The New Dock-yard
D* The Imperial Mews
E* Gostinoi Dvor
F* Bank of Assignats
G* Hôtel de Ville
H* The New Palace Michel
I* The Chateau St Michel
K* The Parade or Exercise House
L* The Little Theatre

M* Private Palace of the Emperor & his Cabinet
N* The Shoving Market
O* Enfans trouvés
P* The Lombard
Q* The Great Theatre
R* Institute of St Catherine
S* Hôpital des Pauvres
T* Semenofskoi Barracks
U* Semenofskoi Hospital
V* Hospital of Oboukoff
W*W* Ismailofskoi Barracks and Hospital
X* Maison d'Accouchement
Y* Kalinkine Hospital
Z* Palace of Catherinof
✱✱ Catherinof or Riga Gate
✱ Triumphal Arch

1 Our Lady of Cazan.   2 The Imperial Library.   3 Smollnoi Convent.

Émile Dupré de Sainte-Maure. *L'hermite en Russie, ou observations sur les moeurs et les usages russes au commencement du XIXe siècle; faisant suite à la collection des moeurs françaises, anglaises, italiennes, espagnoles, etc.* Paris: Pillet aîné, 1829.

Born in Carcassonne, in the Languedoc, in 1772, Dupré de Sainte-Maure had a vaudeville, *La jeunesse de Préville*, performed in Paris in 1805, and in that same year was appointed to a position with Princess Pauline Borghese, Napoleon's sister. Elected deputy of his native département of Aude in 1807, he then served as a sous-préfet in Burgundy. He rallied the Bourbons when they returned to power and occupied functions under both Louis XVIII and Charles X. Before his departure for St. Petersburg, he published, in 1818, a collection of contemporary poetical satires in the Horace-Boileau tradition, entitled *Hier et aujourd'hui*. He died in northern Burgundy, where he had retired, in 1854.

Dupré de Sainte-Maure spent five years in Russia between August 1819 and July 1824. It was during his stay there that he published the *Anthologie russe*, which came out in Paris in 1823. Dedicated, with permission, to Tsar Alexander I, it contains translations of poems by Kantemir, Bobrov, Derzhavin, and Zhukovskii, among others, as well as thirteen fables by Krylov, and an extract from Pushkin's *Ruslan i Liudmila*, published in 1820 when Dupré was in St. Petersburg: it is the first appearance of Pushkin in French. The *Anthologie russe* also contains poems by Dupré himself (including "Les îles de Saint-Pétersbourg," "L'annonce du printemps, à Saint-Pétersbourg," and "Voyage dans les jardins de Pavlovsky") and is illustrated with six lithographs by Langlumé after Aubry, Bichebois, and Loeillet.

L'hermite en Russie is dedicated to Timoléon, ninth duke of Brissac (1775–1848), who served Napoleon and, as the préfet in Dijon, had been Dupré's supervisor when the latter was sous-préfet in Beaune. As he explains in his preface, Dupré did not intend to write about "columns, pilasters, and obelisks" but rather about people and their habits. He is highly critical of other contemporary accounts of Russia for being patronizing towards the Russians, whom he describes as "an eminently good, witty, brave, religious, and charitable people" and hopes that his readers will be able to say, after reading him: "I have been in Russia, I know the Russians."

The title of the work refers, from an allusion in chapter 19, to a nickname the author took— possibly by reference to Catherine the Great and the Hermitage. The book is in three volumes. The 66 chapters, two of which are, in fact, short stories ("Varinka, ou le kabak rouge" and "Les deux crimes, nouvelle russe"), form short vignettes of life in St. Petersburg, arranged in no apparent order.

Unlike other authors, Dupré makes no attempt to give a comprehensive account of the city. His chapter on the Hermitage has little to say about the collections, but rather tries to picture life there at the time of Catherine. When he evokes Peterhof and Tsarskoe Selo, it is in the context of personal excursions.

Some chapters are first-hand accounts of events or festivities: the First of January celebrations, the blessing of the waters, a review on the Champ-de-Mars, the wedding of one of the empress's ladies-in-waiting, a feast at Peterhof, a ball, a sumptuous Petersburg soirée featuring tableaux vivants, a fire, the carnival (with a long quotation from Svin'in's *Description*).

The book contains short portraits of an exiled French composer and the Duke of Serra-Capriola, the Neapolitan ambassador, as well as lively accounts of simple people from St. Petersburg Dupré had contacts with, including maîtres d'hôtel and Finnish chimney-sweeps. What he clearly wants is to convey to his reader a flavor of social life in St. Petersburg: what the salons, family life, the life of the nobility, the art of conversation are like. The book contains observations on topics seldom covered in contemporary accounts of the city: why there are so many bearded people in the streets, the size and splendor of dowries.

The author is not indifferent to larger social issues: there are chapters on religion, women's education, corporal punishment, violent crime, and on the question of the Emancipation. Two separate chapters are devoted to the lottery, while the subject of titles is exposed in the form of a conversation between a Russian and an American.

The book is illustrated throughout with small vignettes, many of which seem purely decorative, without any apparent connection with Petersburg or Russia. Bound with the first volume is a folding map, entitled "Itinéraire de l'hermite," and six vignettes showing the Exchange, the Elagin Palace, the Peter and Paul Fortress, the triumphal gate in honor of Alexander I, the Arsenal, and the Bronze Horseman— which Dupré is almost alone, among contemporary writers on St. Petersburg, in not discussing. Both map and illustrations are credited to Ambroise Tardieu as designer and engraver.

According to Michel Cadot, *L'hermite en Russie* was one of the sources Alexandre Dumas used when writing his "Russian" novel *Le maître d'armes* (1840–41).

Lithograph by Langlumé after Aubry (1822) illustrating Dupré de Sainte-Maure's poem "Les îles de Saint-Pétersbourg,"
from his *Anthologie russe* (1823).

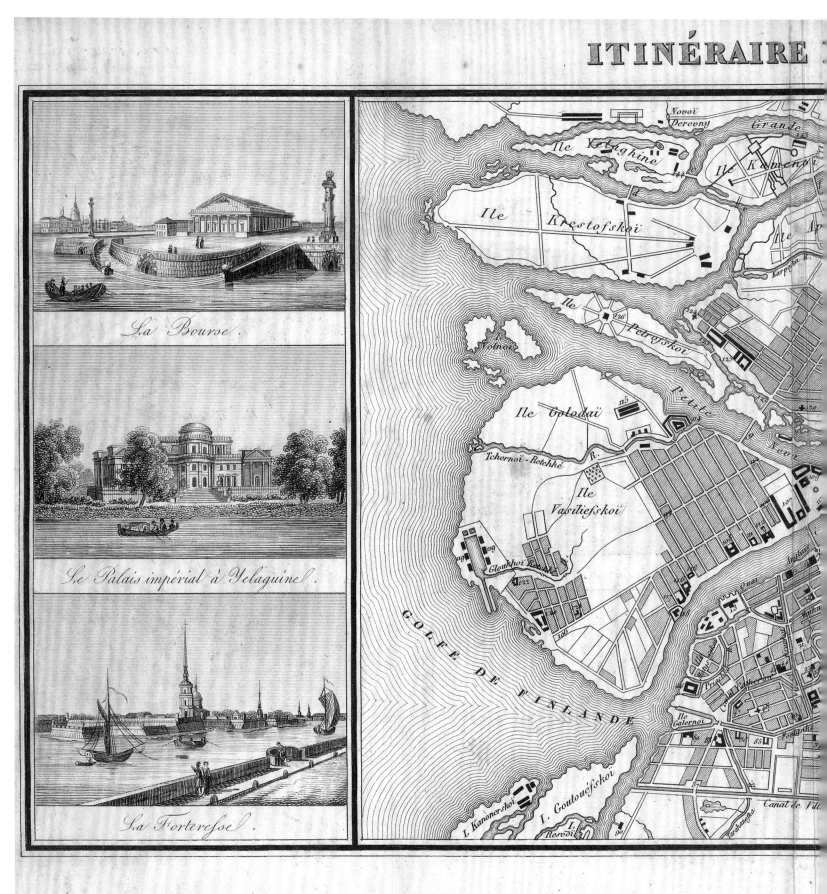

La Bourse.

Le Palais impérial à Yelaguine.

La Forteresse.

A Paris, chez **Pillet** ainé, Editeur de la Collection des Mœurs Françaises, Anglaises, Ecossaises, Irl...

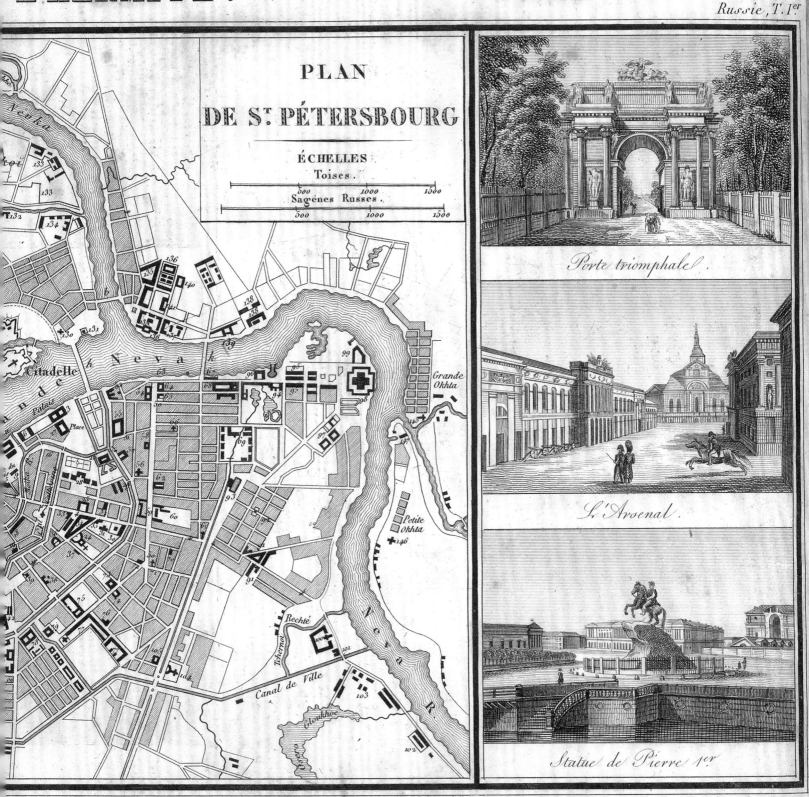

L'HERMITE.

PLAN DE St. PÉTERSBOURG

ÉCHELLES
Toises.

500   1000   1500

Sagènes Russes.

500   1000   1500

Porte triomphale.

L'Arsenal.

Statue de Pierre 1er

Dessiné et gravé par Ambroise Tardieu.

Espagnoles, Grecques, Italiennes et Russes, Rue des Grands Augustins, N.º 7.

Charles Malo. *St-Pétersbourg.* Paris: Marcilly
fils aîné, 1829. (Les capitales de l'Europe.
Promenades pittoresques.)

This small, slim volume, handsomely printed by
Firmin-Didot and bound in yellow boards
ornamented with delicate blind tooling, is the third
in a series of short descriptions of eight European
capitals, the others being Paris, London, Vienna,
Rome, Berlin, Madrid, and Constantinople. Their
author, the Paris-born Charles Malo (1790–1871),
published on a variety of topics—Napoleon,
Benjamin Franklin, Haiti and Santo-Domingo, a
history of the Jews, etc. The Beinecke has the copy of
his verse collection *Le rameau d'or: souvenirs de
littérature contemporaine* that was in the imperial
library at Tsarskoe Selo. In 1832, he founded the
monthly *La France littéraire*, which he edited until
1839 (it had a Russian contributor from St.
Petersburg, Prince Elim Meshcherskii). Of St.
Petersburg, Malo notes that of all European capitals,
it is the one fullest of surprises. The hand-colored
frontispiece shows a view of the Anichkov Palace
from the Fontanka (probably after Makhaev's 1751
rendering), facing north, with Nevsky Prospect in the
background. Commissioned by Elizabeth as a gift to
her morganatic husband Aleksei Razumovsky, the
palace was built by Mikhail Grigorievich Zemtsov in
1741 and completed by Rastrelli after Zemtsov's
death. Presented by Catherine II to Potemkin while
the Tauride Palace was awaiting completion, it then
reverted to the crown. It was famous for its grand
landing on the Fontanka .

   Malo's account is, on the whole, highly
sympathetic, ending with considerations on the
inhabitants of the city. "The distinctive virtues of
Russians are charity and hospitality. There is no
capital in Europe where the latter of these virtues are
carried so far . . . Perhaps in no other country in the
world do friends and relatives give themselves with
such abandon to tender manifestations of mutual
affection." A brief description of the main imperial
residences concludes the book.

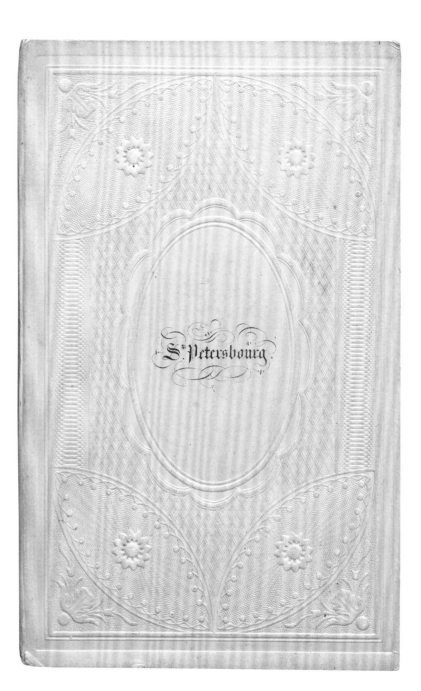

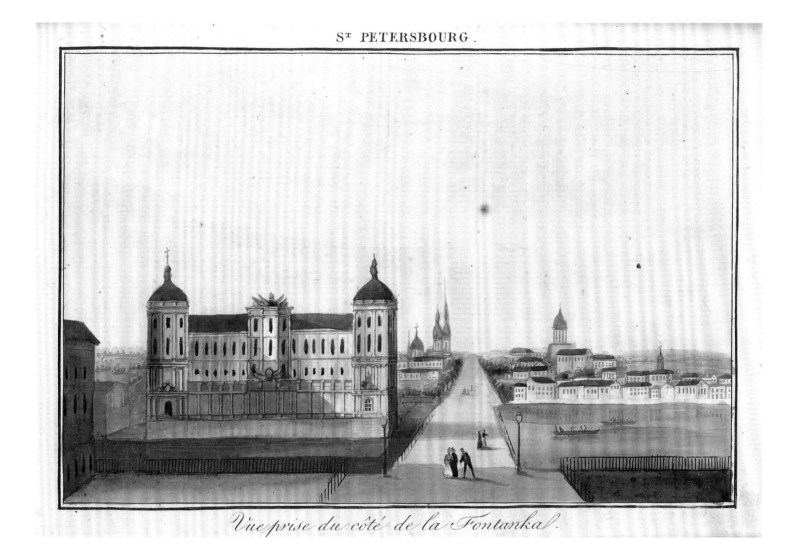

Vue prise du côté de la Fontanka.

Thomas Oldfield. *"Journal of a visit to St Petersburg in 1832."* Manuscript diary, illustrated with pencil or pen-and-ink drawings, some of them retouched with crayon.

This delightful manuscript diary, a recent addition to the James Marshall and Marie-Louise Osborn Collection, is attributed, in pencil, on the title page, to Thomas Oldfield, whose matching initials appear, in ink, next to the illustrations. The diary is written on the recto sides and rubricated on the blank, verso leaves.

Having stopped at Elsinor on the way (like many English visitors), our English tourist arrived at Kronshtadt on 5 June 1832 and spent three weeks in the Russian capital, where he stayed with his friend and compatriot Robert Cattley and his wife, who lived on the English Quay.

Oldfield, evidently a cultivated young man who quotes from Horace and *The tempest*, was a diligent tourist and saw the main sites of the city. He much admires the Bronze Horseman, obtains access to the Winter Palace (eleven and a half lines of text are crossed out of his description), is much impressed with the winter garden of the Tauride Palace, and (like Johnston) notes that the Kazan Cathedral is not quite finished. In the Imperial Public Library, he admires two illuminated missals once in the possession of Mary, Queen of Scots, one of them containing a prayer written in her hand. On the Champ-de-Mars, he sees Nicholas I reviewing troops.

He goes to a performance of a Russian play at the Bolshoi Theater ("the actors appeared to me too dégagés"), sees Molière's *Le médecin malgré lui* at the French Theater (also attended by the tsar in simple military uniform), and hears Weber's *Der Freischütz* at the German Theater. He visits Mr. Law, the English chaplain, and dines at the English Club ("a most inappropriate name by the bye, for only 1/12th of the members are English"), where he finds the food palatable; "but, as I have not graduated in continental kitchens, my opinions in gastronomy must be received with caution."

At a restaurant, he engages in conversation, in French, with a group of Russian women "pleasing in their exterior and apparently ladylike in their manners, but of sickly, cadaverous complexions," which leads to considerations on Russian ladies ("At 27 a Russian belle is quite passée"). "They want the vivacity, animation and esprit of the French, and the gentle feminine attractions of the British fair; but, on the other hand, they surpass the former in ardour, tenderness, and, if I may use the expression, in a capacity for passion, while they exceed the latter in * * * * An affectionate regard for my lovely countrywomen shall prevent my filling up the blank, so that if I cannot blind my judgment, I will at least hold my tongue."

On the way to the Cattleys' house in the country, Oldfield observes and comments on the miserable condition of serfs: "But a brighter day shall dawn, this country shall be regenerated and despite the efforts of despotism, the people shall awake to liberty and life" (he then quotes the famous passage, with the phrase "Dare be free" from Thomas Campbell's *The pleasures of hope*).

Oldfield clearly enjoyed his visit, even though he deplores, almost as soon as he disembarks, "the frequent practice of spitting, with many other κακοθεα [ill manners], better understood than described, are peculiarly offensive to the Englishman," while lamenting the fussiness of the Petersburg police, which causes him to leave the city on 23 June 1832 without his passport. After a final dinner at the residence of the British consul Mr. Booker, he sailed from Kronshtadt on 25 July.

The ten drawings—in ink or pencil, occasionally embellished in crayon—are of "Cronborg" [off the Danish coast]; "Cronstadt batteries and guardship"; "View of St. Petersburg from the English Quay"; "Drotskies"; Russian soldiers; "Russian serfs in 1832"; "Noorina, seat of Robert Cattley Esq."; "Russian carriage and four"; "Russian carriage"; and "Police officer."

VIEW OF ST. PETERSBVRG
FROM THE
ENGLISH QVAY.

The Moika Canal, by Sadovnikov (ca. 1833).

Vasilii Semenovich Sadovnikov. *Panorama de la perspective Nevski / Panorama Nevskogo prospekta*. Hand-colored lithographs on paper by I. and P. Ivanov after Sadovnikov, mounted on linen [St. Petersburg: H. Prévost], [1830]–35. Yale Center for British Art, Paul Mellon Collection.

Born in St. Petersburg, Vasilii Semenovich Sadovnikov (1800–79) belonged to a family of serfs to Princess Evdoksiia Golitsyna, Pushkin's egeria, at whose death in 1838 he was freed. He studied with Voronikhin, the architect of the Kazan Cathedral, and the painters Maksim Nikiforovich Vorobiev (1787–1855) and Aleksei Gavrilovich Venetsianov (1780–1847). After the success of his views of the city in the early 1830s, he received many commissions from the imperial court and noble families to draw their palaces. He remained active at least until the mid-1860s.

Sadovnikov's masterpiece is his panorama of Nevsky Prospect, a 360-degree view of Petersburg's most famous avenue, published in lithographic form after his watercolors. It appears to have been issued in two installments, the earlier, comprising fourteen sheets, for the southwestern side, from the Emperor's Cabinet at the Anichkov Palace to the Admiralty, the latter, comprising sixteen sheets, for the northeastern side, from the Alexander Column to the Anichkov Bridge. When mounted on a single, continuous roll of canvas, as is the Mellon copy, the whole panorama measures 14.5 meters. On the evidence of this copy, it is not an absolutely continuous view, since plates 14 and 15 do not match.

Not every section is labelled. The fourteen sections of the southwestern side are labelled: "His Majesty the Emperor's Cabinet"; "Anichkov Palace"; "Grand Theater (new)"; "Imperial Public Library"; "Great shopping hall (Gostinoi Dvor)"; "City Hall"; "Cathedral of Our Lady of Kazan" (two sections); "House of Countess Strogonoff"; "Police Bridge"; the next three unlabelled; and "View of St. Isaac Square." The sixteen sections of the northeastern side are labelled: "View of the Winter Palace Square with the monument built in honor of Emperor Alexander I with the inscription to Alexander I from a grateful Russia"; the next two unlabelled; "Little Millionaia"; "Police Bridge / House belonging to the Dutch Church"; "Great Stables Street"; "Small Stables Street"; "Kazan Bridge / Engelhardt House"; "Catholic Church; New Street facing the Mihailovsky Palace" [the latter split between this and the following section]; "Armenian Church"; the next

two unlabelled; "Little Garden Street"; the next two unlabelled; and "Anichkov Bridge."

The last section of the southwestern side and the first section of the northeastern side carry the note "Drawn from nature by Sadovnikov" and the name of the lithographers, Ivanov. The two names and the date 1835 are also present in the last section of the northeastern side, in the small black semicircle under the first arch of the Anichkov Bridge.

Nevsky Prospect, which runs from the Admiralty to the Alexander Nevsky Monastery (though the avenue is actually named after the Neva), is almost as old as the city itself, since its construction began as early as 1712 and it was part, as we have seen, of the first plans for the city's development. By the Romantic period, not only was it the chief artery (leading to the road to Moscow), it became the social center of the city. Gogol described it as a microcosm of Petersburg society at the beginning of his short story of the same name, which, published in 1835, is thus exactly contemporary with Sadovnikov's panorama.

Among the many notable buildings featured in this panorama, the Grand Theater, subsequently named the Alexandra Theater in honor of Nicholas I's wife, was of recent completion, the work of Rossi (built in 1828–32). It was there that Gogol's comedy *The government inspector* received its premiere, in the tsar's presence, on 1 May 1836. The Imperial Public Library, the merchant galleries (Gostiny Dvor), and Voronikhin's Kazan Cathedral have already been discussed. The Duma building or city hall is surmounted by a tower whose main function was the detection and announcement of fires. The Stroganov Palace, built by Rastrelli in 1752–54, is one of the oldest buildings on Nevsky Prospect: it has two façades, one on the avenue, the other facing the Moika Canal. On the northeastern side of Nevsky Prospect, the four non-Orthodox churches testify to Petersburg's long traditions of religious tolerance: the Dutch church, hidden behind a neoclassical façade, the work of Paul Jacot, just completed when Sadovnikov drew his view; the Lutheran Church of St. Peter, also quite new (1832), the work of Alexander Brülov (it was used as a swimming-pool from the late 1950s until recent times); the Catholic church of St. Catherine (1762–82), planned and begun by Jean-Baptiste Vallin de La Mothe but completed by Rinaldi; and the Armenian Church, also dedicated to St. Catherine, built by Iurii Fel'ten between 1771 and 1780. Another monument just contemporary with Sadovnikov's panorama is Montferrand's Alexander Column: standing in front of the Winter Palace, it was erected in 1834.

Shops of various kinds are advertised by signs as often as not in both cyrillic and roman characters. There are several hatters, clothes merchants for men or women, bookstores, drugstores (including an "English Apothocary" [sic]), tailors, lithographers, hairdressers, caterers, and restaurants. Other stores sell spectacles, clocks, embroidery, furniture, perfumes, French pottery, jewels, chocolates. Some of the more elaborate stores have more recherché names: "A la renommée," "Au fidèle berger," "Magazin hellandaise" [sic], "Magazin italien," "Au magasin de Paris: Papeterie [?], Bonbons, Nouveautés, Etrennes." There is a notary, while the dentist advertises himself in French only, and towards the top of the southwestern side, one can see the entrance to a bathhouse. On the other side, at the bend of the Moika, an interesting sign, on the second floor, reads "Salon d'exposition de la société d'encouragement des artistes russes."

The names seen on the signs, also often in both cyrillic and roman characters, reveal a highly diverse ethnic mix: Puls, Churkin, Pelletier, Reichardt, Peters, Wispolskii, Xavier, Mauer, Formann, Goese, Verdier (hairdresser), Elers, Martin Boll, Gaubert (lithographer), Renaud (hatter), Rode, Bellizard (bookseller), Botou (tailor), Kenman (clockmaker), Devant [&] Wendt, Amato, Falers, Walter, Jacobs, Keman (jeweller), Markewitsch (tailor), Beggrow (lithographer), Friemann, Guedd.

Probably the two most famous public establishments pictured, both on the northeastern side, are the Engelhardt House and Wolff & Béranger. The former hosted balls and masquerades (it is the setting of Lermontov's play *The masked ball*), but also contained a concert hall (where Liszt, Berlioz, and Wagner performed), a hotel, and a deluxe restaurant. Wolff & Béranger, now called the Literary Café, was patronized by a fashionable clientèle, including Pushkin, who met his second Danzas there on his way to his fatal duel with d'Anthès on 27 January 1837.

If not as complete a sample as the one evoked, at different moments of the day, in Gogol's story, the people represented nevertheless show a wide gallery of St. Petersburg society: noblemen and well-to-do citizens in their calèches (two are seen greeting each other), officers, soldiers, tradespeople of various kinds: a wine merchant, a water carrier, delivery boys carrying baskets of food or pastry on their heads—such a pastry boy was killed by the first of the two bombs thrown at Alexander II when he was assassinated on 1 March 1881. In the Anichkov Palace section, an important personage is saluted by several people in the crowd. A couple is seen walking with their poodle in the Kazan Cathedral section; in another, a woman is surrounded by several dogs. A hay cart is one of the vehicles crossing the Anichkov Bridge. A notable feature is the conspicuous presence of the army: guards on sentry duty in front of official buildings, groups of soldiers, detachments marching, a military parade in the distance on Admiralty Prospect.

A great variety of vehicles can be seen: a well-filled stagecoach, open and closed carriages of varying size and splendor, the more imposing drawn by four horses, simple drozhki for private or public use, as is apparently the case of the four standing in front of the Rusca Portico. The wooden pavement, characteristic of pre-revolutionary St. Petersburg, is alternatively scrubbed, swept, washed, and repaired in various sections (only the sidewalks were in stone).

The coloring of the Mellon copy is likely to have been realized, if not by the original owner, at least for him or her. The Yale Center for British Art has a second copy of the fourteen sections of the southwestern side, also from the collection of Paul Mellon, in which the coloring is strikingly different. That copy is described in J.R. Abbey's *Life in England in aquatint and lithography, 1770–1860* (Folkestone: Dawsons of Pall Mall, 1972; no. 520).

Малая Миліонная
Petite millianne.

Полицейскій мостъ
Pont de Police.

Голандскій Церковный домъ
Maison app.^{nt} a l'Eglise Hollandaise.

Большая Конюшенная
Grande rue des Ecuries.

John Dunn Gardner. "Journal of my travels on the Continent." Manuscript diary, 1835–70.

John Dunn Gardner (1811–1903) was of Charteris, Cambridgeshire, where he served as High Sheriff for a while. He is remembered chiefly as a book collector: his large library was sold by Sotheby and Wilkinson in two sessions in 1854 and 1875. He is the author of two books, *Ascent and tour of Mont Blanc and passage of the Col du Géant, between Sept. 2nd and 7th 1850*, privately printed by Charles Whittingham in Chiswick in 1851, and *The Ionian Islands in relation to Greece, with suggestions for advancing our trade with the Turkish countries of the Adriatic and the Danube*, which went through two editions in 1859. He was above all an avid traveller, as his journals show (one of them is in the Princeton University Library). The two volumes in the James Marshall and Marie-Louise Osborn Collection contain diary accounts of twelve different expeditions, mostly in Western Europe.

Gardner went to Russia in 1837–38 in the course of a trip that took him first to Rotterdam, then to Bonn, and through Germany, to Poland and Estonia. He arrived in St. Petersburg on 13 December and left on 13 February for Moscow. Remarkably, this diary contains no description of the city or any account of Gardner's activities during the two months of his stay. It is possible that he kept a separate notebook that has yet to surface. The Osborn manuscript is limited to the following:

"The approach to St. Petersburg is unstriking till you reach the bronze triumphal arch, & then everything looks so scattered & wild that no stranger believes he is in a city; 30 or 40 verstes before reaching to city are some German colonies, established by Peter the Great; each is composed of a few houses arranged in a row, making a tiny village; each house is isolated, being a square or nearly so, one story high with a window in front, built of wood & painted a sandy yellow color; on each side at a little interval is an office; every house of the colony has the owner's name in German & Russian with the number of the house marked up; the colonists wear the dress of Germany, i.e. they dont wear the coarse pelisse with the girdle, the furred cap, & beard of the Russian poor; the land & habitation are given them, or rather, they hold it, on conditions; the houses are of wood like all out of the cities, but they have a happy look, with signs of wealth; some keep their calèche; they find a good market for their produce at Petersburg; after all the number of colonists is very limited, & presents to the eye but a formal, uninteresting look."

Two views of the English Quay, by Sadovnikov (ca. 1833).

Astolphe de Custine. *La Russie en 1839.* Paris: Amyot, 1843.

Astolphe, marquis de Custine (1790–1857) was the grandson of a guillotined general of the French Revolution who had taken part in the battle of Yorktown. His own father too was guillotined in 1794 at the age of 24. This personal experience of revolutionary violence forms the background, and, in fact, is explicitly recounted as a preface to Custine's account of Russia. Yet, for his resulting monarchist politics and fervent Catholicism, Custine was as openly gay as the age permitted, living with his English friend Edward Sainte-Barbe in a quasi marriage. A "half man of letters," in his friend Heine's unkind words, he published several novels, had a play produced at the Comédie-Française, and wrote books on England and on Spain under Ferdinand VII. Other friendships included Chateaubriand, Balzac, Hugo, Rahel Varnhagen and her husband, Mickiewicz, Meyerbeer, and Chopin.

Custine's 1839 trip to Russia was spurred by the triumph of Tocqueville's *De la démocratie en Amérique*, where democracy is represented as the ineluctable political evolution of advanced societies. Custine may have hoped that Russia was the proof that enlightened despotism was an equally viable system. He was also hoping, on a more personal level, to be able to intercede in favor of his Polish lover Ignatz Gurowski and his brothers, whose estates had been confiscated by the tsar.

Having left Paris on 15 May, Custine arrived in Petersburg on 10 July 1839. He remained there until 3 August, then visited Moscow, Jaroslav, Nizhni-Novgorod, returning on 8 September to St. Petersburg, where he spent another two weeks. He crossed the East Prussian border on 26 September.

What Custine discovered, or believed he had discovered in Russia, turned out to be of a totally different nature from what he had expected to find: a country dominated by fear of a tyrannical power served by an implacable bureaucracy, in other words a police state. Reluctant at first to publish his impressions, he did so after four years of discreet work. The success of the book was considerable. The 3,000 copies of the first printing sold out. Four pirate editions came out in Brussels before the second edition appeared in Paris. The first English edition, entitled *The Empire of the Czar,* was issued in the same year, as was the first German edition; both were reprinted the following year. In Russia, Custine's book was banned

at once. Yet it was widely read in the original, and greeted with open indignation by most and secret admiration by some liberal thinkers such as Alexander Herzen. Furious at first, Nicholas I is reported to have grown to like it— or at least some portions, which he read to his family. An abbreviated Russian edition eventually came out in 1910.

Despite its misleadingly conversational form— a series of thirty-one letters supposedly sent in the course of the journey, all but one to an unnamed friend—, *La Russie en 1839* is a carefully constructed pamphlet, in which everything converges towards a denunciation of absolutism and a plea for liberty. Custine's account of St. Petersburg is in line with this general concept. The city is viewed as the mirror image of the "empire of façades" (to borrow Herzen's phrase), a gigantic Potemkin village. The artificially created capital, "without roots or history" ("a painted up marsh, plastered up swamp"), hides a social reality that is a permanent conspiracy against truth. Similarly, the neoclassical style of the palaces is interpreted as decorative, theatrical— an architectural form of deceit. A spectacular feast at Peterhof is contrasted with the secrecy surrounding an accident that caused the deaths of an untold number of victims. Despite this dark picture (not too different, paradoxically, from the one presented by Nekrasov, Gogol, and Dostoyevsky), Custine is not insensitive to the beauty of the White Nights, admits that the city is "infinitely picturesque," and, while claiming that the light in the Hermitage is not flattering to the paintings, grants that the Rembrandt room is the finest he has ever seen.

The first complete modern English translation of Custine, with the revealing subtitle "A journey through eternal Russia," was published in 1989 with a foreword by Daniel Boorstin and an introduction by George Kennan. In the words of the latter, "even if we admit that *La Russie en 1839* was not a very good book about Russia in 1839, we are confronted with the fact that it was an excellent book, probably in fact the best of books, about the Russia of Joseph Stalin." Beside this revealing, if questionable modern appraisal is the resentment Custine's work continues to inspire in Russia, as recently evidenced by his appearance in the film *The Russian Ark*.

LA RUSSIE
EN 1839

PAR

LE MARQUIS DE CUSTINE

« Respectez surtout les étrangers, de quelque qualité, de quelque
« rang qu'ils soient, et si vous n'êtes pas à même de les combler
« de présents, prodiguez-leur au moins des marques de bienveil-
« lance, puisque de la manière dont ils sont traités dans un pays
« dépend le bien et le mal qu'ils en disent en retournant dans
« le leur. »

(Extrait des conseils de Vladimir Monomaque à ses enfants en 1126.
Histoire de l'Empire de Russie, par Karamsin, t. II, p. 205.)

TOME PREMIER

PARIS
LIBRAIRIE D'AMYOT, ÉDITEUR
6, RUE DE LA PAIX
1843

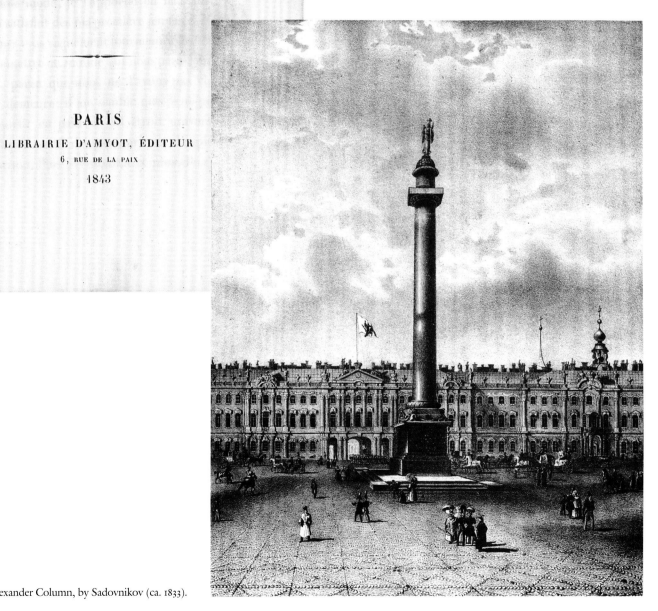

The Alexander Column, by Sadovnikov (ca. 1833).

André Durand. *Excursion pittoresque et archéologique en Russie par le Hâvre, Hambourg, Lubeck, Saint-Petersbourg, Moscou, Nijni-Novgorod, Yaroslaw et Kasan, exécutée en 1839, sous la direction de M. Anatole de Démidoff. Dessins faits d'après nature et lithographiés à deux teintes.* Paris: Gihaut frères [1842–48].

Anatolii Nikolaevich Demidov, Prince of San Donato (1812–70), was the second son of a wealthy dilettante (Granville calls him "one of the wealthiest private individuals in Russia") who lived mostly in Paris and Florence. The Demidov family owed its fortune to Peter the Great and held iron and copper mines in the Ural region. Anatolii Nikolaevich was raised in Paris. In 1837, after spending a few years in the diplomatic service, he launched a scientific expedition, chiefly geological, to the Ukraine and Crimea. The results were published in Paris under the title *Esquisse d'un voyage dans la Russie méridionale et la Crimée en 1837*. The book, which was the work of various collaborators, was reissued, in its definitive form, in 1841–42, at Demidov's expense, as *Voyage dans la Russie méridionale et la Crimée, par la Hongrie, la Valachie et la Moldavie*, illustrated with lithographs by Denis-Auguste-Marie Raffet.

Demidov subsequently sponsored this "picturesque excursion" from Le Havre to Kazan by André Durand (1807–67), a painter from Normandy, who between June and November 1839 realized a series of views in collaboration with Raffet (who is credited for the figures), which were later published as duotone folio-size lithographs. The nineteen plates devoted to St. Petersburg form two series. The first, dated June–July 1839, shows Kronshtadt, the police tower on Moskovskii Prospect, the Peter and Paul Cathedral, the Winter Palace and Admiralty, St. Isaac Square with the Bronze Horseman (with the name of Catherine the Great accidentally omitted on the pedestal), the house of Peter the Great, Nevsky Prospect, the Hermitage, the Admiralty, St. Nicholas Cathedral, the Alexander Nevsky Monastery, a village church near Tsarskoe Selo, two sites specifically associated with the Demidov family, the so-called "Comptoir Demidoff" on Vasilievsky Island and a "maison de bienfaisance" near the Magasins impériaux. The second series, dated October–November 1839, shows the Kazan Cathedral, the Smolny Monastery, the Palace Embankment, the Alexandra Theater, and the Schlussenburg Fortress on Lake Ladoga.

The view of Nevsky Prospect from the Police Bridge shows the characteristic wooden pavement perfected in 1832 by the engineer Guriev, which remained in place in the elegant parts of St. Petersburg until the Revolution.

In 1840, in Florence, Demidov married Princess Mathilde, the daughter of Jerome Bonaparte, Napoleon I's youngest brother. The princely couple briefly visited Russia, settled in Paris, and spent a year in St. Petersburg in 1842–43 before returning to Italy. They were separated in 1846 after an intervention from Nicholas I, who sided with Mathilde against her abusive and unfaithful husband, whom he banned from travelling to Paris.

This photograph was published in
Louis Réau's *Saint-Pétersbourg* (1913).

ALEXANDRE DUMAS

DE

PARIS A ASTRAKAN

NOUVELLES IMPRESSIONS DE VOYAGE

PREMIÈRE SÉRIE

PARIS
LIBRAIRIE NOUVELLE
BOULEVARD DES ITALIENS, 15
—
A. BOURDILLIAT ET Cᵉ, ÉDITEURS
—
La traduction et la reproduction sont réservées
—
1860

The Exchange, by Sadovnikov (ca. 1833).

Alexandre Dumas. *De Paris à Astrakan: nouvelles impressions de voyage. Première série.* Paris: Librairie nouvelle; Bourdillat et Cie, 1860.

When he went to Russia in June 1858, Dumas was hardly an unknown figure: a famous, prolific playwright, an even more famous novelist, author of *Les trois mousquetaires* (1844) and *Le comte de Monte Cristo* (1845–46), and also, from a Russian viewpoint, *Le maître d'armes* (1840–41) based on the life of the Decembrist Ivan Aleksandrovich Annenkov (1802–78) and his French fiancée: it made Dumas persona non grata in Russia during the remainder of Nicholas I's reign (although Dumas reports with relish that the tsarina was caught reading it by her husband).

Dumas's account first appeared in forty-three installments in his own weekly magazine, entitled *Le Monte-Cristo*, and in book form in Naumburg and Brussels in 1858, then in Paris two years later. The serialization was continued in 1861 in *Le Constitutionnel* and a complete edition came out four years later. As the stamp on the title page shows, the Beinecke copy of the first volume of the 1860 Paris edition (the other two volumes are missing) comes from the imperial library at Tsarskoe Selo, along with ninety-two other Alexandre Dumas titles in the Beinecke. The size of the collection (which does not include *Le maître d'armes*) is a sign of Dumas's reputation in Russia at the time. Following the dispersal and sale of a large part of the tsars' library in the years following the Revolution, those Dumas editions were acquired by the New York collector Frank Altschul, whose magnificent library was particularly rich in French books, and subsequently donated by him to Yale.

By his own account, Dumas went to Russia at the invitation of a prominent member of the St. Petersburg nobility, Count Grigorii Kuchelev-Bezborodko (ca. 1830–76), who owned a palace on the Neva, across from the Smolny Monastery. He was also accompanied by the genre painter Jean-Pierre Moynet (1819–76). The pretext of the trip was to attend the wedding of the count's sister with another friend, the celebrated Scottish spiritualist medium Daniel Dunglas [not Douglas, as Dumas has it] Home (1833–86), a sometime Connecticut resident. Home's marriage to Alexandrina de Krol, the sister of Countess Kuchelev-Bezborodko, took place in St. Petersburg on 1 August (new style) 1858. Dumas arrived in the Russian capital on 22 June and left on 3 August for Moscow. His trip took him all the way to Astrakhan on the Caspian Sea, and he returned to France by boat via Trebizond and Constantinople.

Dumas's narrative mirrors in many ways the larger-than-life, multifaceted personality of its author. It is unabashedly autobiographical and written in a quasi-conversational tone which contrasts with Custine's lapidary, elegant formality. Although two-thirds of the book are supposedly devoted to St. Petersburg, Dumas's survey of the city, even when presented as an actual promenade, seems to be above all a pretext for historical anecdotes and portraits of the great figures of Russian history, most of whom could easily inhabit a Dumas novel. Consequently, one is not surprised to see Grigorii Orlov likened to Porthos and Buckingham, while the name of d'Anthès, Pushkin's duel adversary, is spelled like that of the hero of *Le comte de Monte Cristo*. On the other hand, a noteworthy feature of the book is the prominence given to literature. Pushkin not only receives his due, but Dumas quotes him liberally (including *The Bronze Horseman*). He also quotes at length from Lermontov, Ryleev, and Nekrasov.

Art and architecture do not receive as much attention. Dumas is particularly critical of the green color of roofs and, like Custine, indulges in flippantly dismissive judgments: "St. Petersburg's great curse is imitation. Its houses are imitations of Berlin; its parks are an imitation of Versailles, Fontainebleau, and Rambouillet; its Neva is an imitation of the Thames, thawing notwithstanding."

On the other hand, Dumas is attentive to social questions (he visits a Petersburg prison and tells the life stories of several of its inmates). Nor, unlike Théophile Gautier, does he shy away from political considerations. He thus makes it clear that one of the purposes of his journey was "to attend at the same time that vast operation of the freeing of forty-five million serfs." While the Emancipation is not further discussed in the book, there are scattered references to serfdom, and it can be noted that Dumas occasionally uses the term "slave," no doubt a calculated choice on his part, given his own ethnic background. He also published in Brussels, separately from his travel account, the book *Lettres de Saint-Pétersbourg*, dealing specifically with this question: it was reprinted in Paris in 1865 as part of the first complete edition of Dumas's travels to Russia, under the general title *Impressions de voyage . . . En Russie. Lettres sur le servage en Russie*.

The Senate, seen from St. Isaac Bridge, by Sadovnikov (ca. 1833).

Théophile Gautier. *Voyage en Russie.* Paris: Charpentier, 1867.

In Henry James's words, "Gautier's winter in Russia was apparently one of the happiest seasons of his life." The French Romantic poet, novelist, and art critic spent the winter of 1858–59 in Russia. He stayed mostly in St. Petersburg, where he was from mid-October 1858 until the end of January 1859, and again in February–March of that year, having visited Moscow in between. He was then involved in a project of a luxury publication, "Artistic treasures of ancient and modern Russia," to be issued by subscription, under the official patronage of Tsar Alexander II, and illustrated with heliographic reproductions of photographs by Richebourg, a pupil of Daguerre, Gautier being in charge of the accompanying text. In the event, and despite a second visit in the summer and early fall of 1861 to resurrect the project, only the first four fascicles of the *Trésors d'art,* dealing with St. Isaac and Tsarskoe Selo, were published (the fifth was printed but not issued). However, sketches of Russia had been commissioned by *Le moniteur universel,* the conservative Paris daily to which Gautier contributed art and theater reviews. These were published between October 1858 and December 1861. Other chronicles, dealing with the theater and ballet, appeared in the *Journal de Saint-Pétersbourg,* and more appeared in other periodicals, such as the *Revue nationale et étrangère.*

Gautier first intended to collect only some of his sketches in a book to be entitled "Saint-Pétersbourg." He eventually expanded the scope of the publication and his *Voyage en Russie* was published in two volumes in 1867; the date printed on the outside wrappers is, however, 1866. Of the first and by far longest part, "L'hiver en Russie: esquisses de voyage," 12 chapters (out of a total of 21) are devoted to the imperial capital. The second, "L'été en Russie," contains only one chapter, "Le Volga" (which, bizarrely, was treated as a masculine noun in French well into the nineteenth century), an account of a trip from Tver to Nizhni-Novgorod.

While Custine's account was political and Dumas's autobiographical, Gautier, in keeping with his literary doctrine of art for art's sake, aims at objectivity. Gautier's is an unapologetically picturesque description of the city in winter, "a verbal symphony on the theme of frost," in the words of Henry James, who reviewed the first American edition for the *Nation* in 1874. Gautier's account also retains the form and quasi-conversational tone of the feuilleton; nor is he shy of repetitions: thus the cigar-loving narrator reminds his readers three times that smoking is not permitted in the streets of St. Petersburg—a measure obviously dictated by the fear of fires.

If this account, which eschews any mention of politics and social change (a remarkable omission considering that Alexander II's Emancipation Act took place between Gautier's two Russian visits), could easily be accused of superficiality, its redeeming feature is its precise yet poetic descriptions of people and places. This is particularly the case of the chapter on the recently completed St. Isaac (the text is, in fact, reprinted from the first of the "Art treasures" fascicles). It is not surprising that the art critic should devote a long chapter to the Hungarian painter Mihaly Zichy, who was official court painter from 1859 until 1872, and his circle of artists known as the Friday Society. Nor is it surprising, on the part of the father of *Giselle,* that the chapter on St. Petersburg theaters dwells on the perfection (already well above Western European standards) of the ballet company, then headed by the great Lyonnais dancer and choreographer Jules Perrot. The same chapter contains a detailed account of performances by the African-American actor Ira Frederick Aldridge, whom he applauded in St. Petersburg as Othello and Lear. Another chapter is devoted entirely to Pugni's and Perrot's ballet *Éolide, ou la dryade,* which Gautier saw at the Mariinsky Theater.

The Peter and Paul Fortress and Cathedral, by Sadovnikov (ca. 1833).

The État Major seen from the Moika Canal, by Sadovnikov (ca. 1833).

Giuseppe Verdi. Autograph letters, signed, to Francesco Maria Piave. [St. Petersburg] 14 December 1861 and [January 1862]

Verdi, at 47, was at the height of celebrity, his works regularly performed in Russia, when he received a commission from the Imperial Theater in St. Petersburg in December 1860. It was transmitted by the famous tenor Enrico Tamberlick (1820–89), reportedly the first Manrico to interpolate a high C in "Di quella pira." The composer was in semi-retirement, while being pressed by Cavour into Italian politics. Yet he agreed, though his first suggestion for a subject, Victor Hugo's iconoclastic *Ruy Blas* (in which the Queen of Spain falls in love with a servant disguised as a nobleman) was not received well by the censors. Verdi then selected the Duke of Rivas's 1835 melodrama *Don Alvaro o la fuerza del sino*. For a librettist, he turned to Francesco Maria Piave (1810–76), his collaborator of nearly twenty years, notably on *Ernani*, *Rigoletto*, and *La traviata*. Piave spent the summer of 1861 drafting the poem, sending batches of text to Verdi, and visiting him at his estate of Busseto. The music was composed between September and mid-November, after which the composer and his wife, Giuseppina Strepponi, set out for Russia by way of Paris, Berlin, and Warsaw.

Verdi arrived in the Russian capital on 6 December and settled in a grand apartment leased for him and his wife by the Imperial Theater. Verdi was still at work revising the music, as evidenced by his letter to Piave dated 14 December, in which he acknowledges the receipt of the text sent by Piave for the cantabile section of the act 4 duet between Alvaro and Carlo, while finding it "almost impossible to set to music." He supplies his own lines instead ("Do what you will with them"). They are in fact very close to the final version of the passage ("Le minaccie, i fieri accenti . . .") quoted in the prelude (and retained in the overture written for the 1869 Milan premiere). Verdi also mentions that the rehearsals have not started yet. They were, in fact, postponed indefinitely by the illness of Emma La Grua, the Sicilian soprano engaged for the part of Leonora, as Verdi reports in the letter he wrote to Piave in early January. In the meantime Verdi kept making alterations to the score, here sending additional text for Piave to versify for inclusion in the third duet between Alvaro and Carlo in act 3, as he fears the baritone's part is unequal to the tenor's. "For three days," he adds, "we have had 20 degrees of cold, but inside 14 degrees of heat: it's marvellous!"

The premiere was eventually postponed until the following winter. Verdi and his wife visited Moscow before returning to Paris. After a trip to London for the premiere of his *Inno delle nazioni* (his first collaboration with Boito), Verdi was back in St. Petersburg on 24 September 1862, still making changes to *La forza del destino* (and visiting Moscow again for the premiere of *Il trovatore*). The French soprano Caroline Douvry-Barbot was engaged to sing Leonora after her success in *Un ballo in maschera* in the Russian capital. The premiere of the new opera took place at the Mariinsky Theater on 10 November. The rest of the cast included, in addition to Tamberlick, the baritone Francesco Graziani, the bass Gian Francesco Angelini, another French singer, Constance Nantier-Didier, as Preziosilla, and, in the small part of the Alcade, the bass Ignazio Marini, who, twenty-three years before, had premiered at La Scala the title role of Verdi's first opera, *Oberto*. Tsar Alexander II and his wife attended the fourth performance, and Verdi was presented with the cross of St. Stanislas. He and his wife remained in St. Petersburg until 9 December.

In its Petersburg version, *La forza del destino* is a significantly different work from the one we know, which incorporates Verdi's revisions for the 1869 Milan premiere. In particular, he reduced the taxing tenor role, and the final scene was completely rewritten, a serene trio replacing the original melodramatic ending, at the conclusion of which Alvaro threw himself from a rock after cursing the human race.

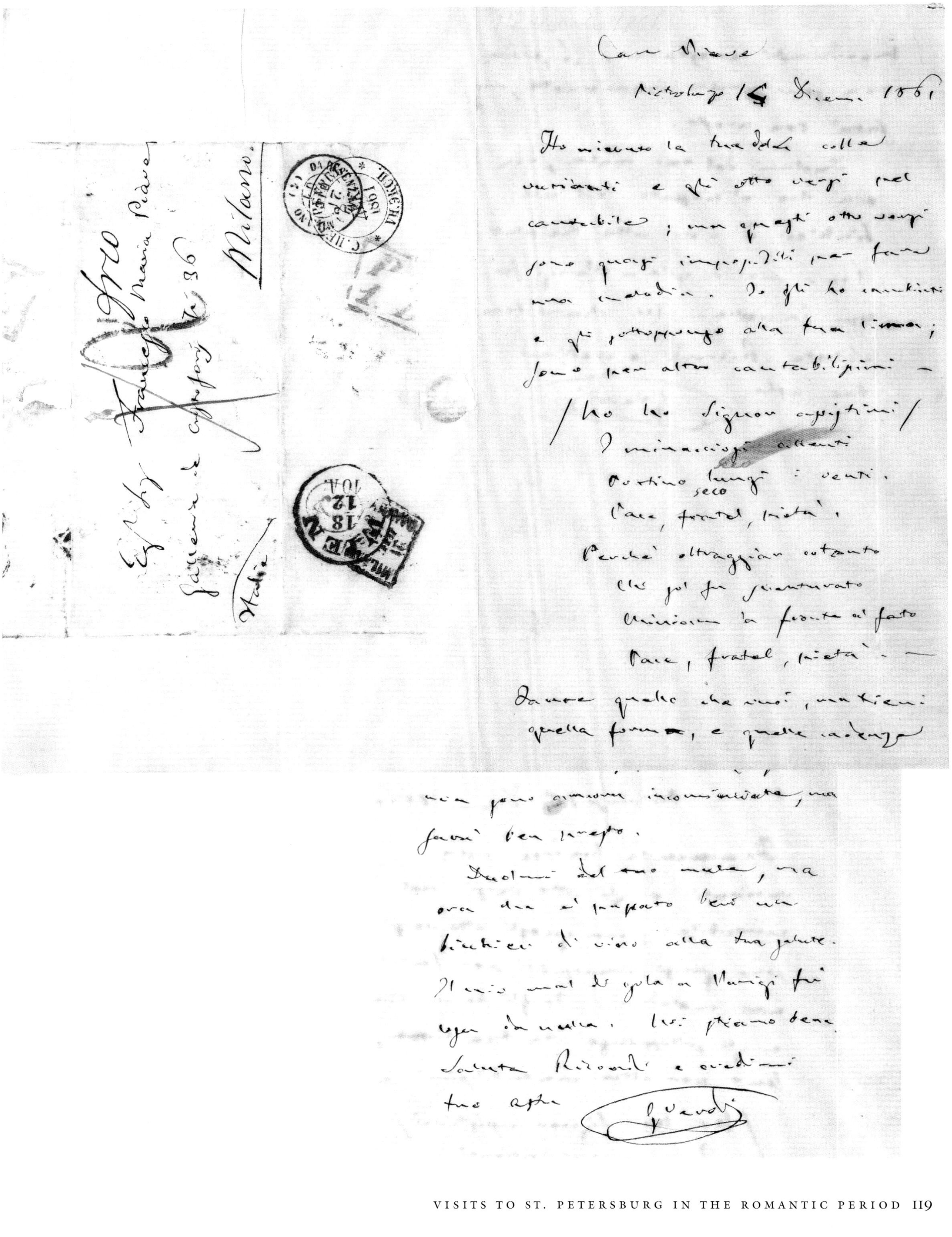

III. From the Twentieth Century

Andrey Bely. *Peterburg.* Petrograd [Tip. M. M. Stasiuvlevicha] 1916.

Andrey Bely (Bely being the Russian for white) was the pseudonym of Boris Nikolaevich Bugaev. Born in 1880, he was graduated from Moscow University (where his father was dean) as a natural scientist in 1903. He was much influenced by his contacts with the mystical philosopher Vladimir Solov'ev and by the occultist anthropologist Rudolph Steiner.

Petersburg, Bely's second novel, is not only his prose masterpiece but, in the opinion of many (Nabokov among them), one of the greatest Russian novels of the twentieth century. It was drafted in 1911 and submitted to the journal *Russkaia Mysl'* (Russian Thought), which rejected it. It was serialized in 1913–14 in the periodical *Sirin* and issued in book form by the Petersburg publisher of the same name in 1916. Bely revised the novel in 1921 when living in Berlin. This revised version, shorter than the original by a third, was published in that city in 1922 and subsequently reprinted in Russia in 1928 and 1935 with cuts imposed by the Soviet censors.

At once a novel including history and an allegory, *Petersburg* is situated in late September and early October 1905. It coincides with the official termination of the war with Japan, which Russia lost after the fall of Port Arthur the previous January, and the revolutionary events that marked the year: the bloody demonstrations of 9/22 January— an event Bely witnessed, though it is not specifically evoked in the novel— and the various strikes that followed, resulting in Nicholas II's signing of the liberal manifesto of 17/30 October. The complex plot revolves around a bomb destined for Apollon Apollonovich Ableukhov, a senator who has just been tapped for a government position. The bomb is delivered to his son Nikolai, who has revolutionary sympathies, and who accidentally sets off the mechanism that will cause it to explode within twenty-four hours. Other characters with significant roles in the novel are Sofia Petrovna, the woman Nikolai Apollonovich has been involved with, and her husband Sergei Sergeevich Likhutin; the revolutionary agitator Alexander Ivanovich Dudkin and the sinister double agent Lippachenko; Anna Petrovna, Senator Ableukhov's estranged wife, who returns to Petersburg that very day. One of the key scenes of the novel takes place during a masked ball; a suicide attempt and a murder precede the final explosion in the senator's office, which in turn prompts the spiritual reawakening of Nikolai Apollonovich.

As the title implies, the city of Petersburg can be considered the main character of the novel. Many of the settings, such as the Summer Garden, are familiar; others, like the location of the Ableukhov house, are deliberately kept vague. Throughout the book, the Bronze Horseman figures as a constant presence, with many references to Pushkin's poem. As in Pushkin, the statue of Peter the Great is more than a symbol of the city: it takes on a life of his own— like that of the Commander in *Don Giovanni*—, likened to the Flying Dutchman of the legend, and appearing to Dudkin in a terrifying hallucination, similar to the one that befalls Pushkin's Evgeny.

After spending the years 1921–23 in Berlin, Bely returned to Russia, where he led a semi-retired life while continuing to publish poetry, novels (the third, and second most important, *Kotik Letaev*, came out in 1922), and memoirs until his death in 1934.

Nabokov famously ranked *Petersburg* among his personal favorites in twentieth-century fiction, along with *Ulysses*, Kafka's *Metamorphosis*, and Proust's *A la recherche du temps perdu* (the first half only). A few interesting, coincidental similarities can be noted between the first edition of *Petersburg* and that of *Ulysses* (1922): the unusual quarto format, the undecorated cover (blank in the case of *Ulysses*), the absence of a running title, the rather neutral choice of type. Unlike Joyce, Bely favors chapter titles and even introduces subtitles; like him, he makes abundant and original use of punctuation.

ПЕТЕРБУРГЪ

РОМАНЪ

АНДРЕЯ БѢЛАГО

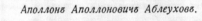

Аполлонъ Аполлоновичъ Аблеуховъ.

Аполлонъ Аполлоновичъ Аблеуховъ былъ весьма почтеннаго рода: онъ имѣлъ своимъ предкомъ Адама. И это не главное: несравненно важнѣе здѣсь то, что благородно рожденный предокъ былъ Симъ, то-есть самъ прародитель семитскихъ, хесситскихъ и краснокожихъ народностей.

Здѣсь мы сдѣлаемъ переходъ къ предкамъ не столь удаленной эпохи.

Эти предки (такъ кажется) проживали въ киргизъ-кайсацкой ордѣ, откуда въ царствованіе императрицы Анны Іоанновны доблестно поступилъ на русскую службу мирза Абъ-Лай, прапрадѣдъ сенатора, получившій при христіанскомъ крещеніи имя Андрея и прозвище Ухова. Такъ о семъ выходцѣ изъ нѣдръ монгольскаго племени распространяется Гербовникъ Россійской Имперіи. Для краткости послѣ былъ превращенъ Абъ-Лай-Уховъ въ Аблеухова просто.

Этотъ прапрадѣдъ, какъ говорятъ, оказался истокомъ рода.

. . . .

Сѣрый лакей съ золотымъ галуномъ пуховкою стряхивалъ пыль съ письменнаго стола; въ открытую дверь заглянулъ колпакъ повара.

— „Самъ-то, вишь, всталъ...“
— „Обтираются одеколономъ, скоро пожалуютъ къ кофію...“

7

VUE DE St PETERSBOURG.

ВИДЪ ДВОРЦА ПЕТРА Iго ✦ VUE DU PALAIS DE PIERRE Ier
въ лѣтнемъ садy au jardin d'été.

Издатель А.Прево Éditeur H. Prévost

The Marble Palace and
Summer Garden (scene of an
episode in Bely's *Petersburg*),
by Sadovnikov (ca. 1833).

Sholem Asch. *Peterburg.* Holograph manuscript, ca. 1928–29.

The most prominent and prolific Yiddish writer of his age, Sholem Asch was born in the small Polish shtetl of Kutno in 1880, then part of the Russian empire. He moved to Warsaw in 1899 and gained attention with the novella *Dos shtetl* (The little town, 1904). His sketches of Jewish life were soon published in the Petersburg Yiddish journal *Der Fraynd*. Of the nine plays between 1904 and 1914, the best known, if also the most controversial, *Got fun nekome* (God of vengeance), was successfully premiered in St. Petersburg in 1907 by the company of the popular actor Nikolai N. Khodotov, in a Russian translation by Osip Dymov. After being expelled from the city as a Jew, Asch was able to attend the first performance thanks to the last-minute intervention of the tsar's uncle.

In 1914, Asch immigrated to America, becoming a citizen in 1920. In 1925, he resettled in Europe, first in Paris, then in Nice. Alarmed by the rise of the Nazis, he played an active role in denouncing them, especially through the PEN Club, while promoting the Zionist cause.

Peterburg (1929) is first in a cycle of three novels Asch devoted to the question of Jewish identity seen in the context of the crises of Eastern Europe between 1905 and 1920. The novel evokes pre-revolutionary Russia from the viewpoint of successful and assimilated Jewish milieux.

The novel takes place chiefly in the years 1911–13. Nina, the daughter of the ambitious and successful defense lawyer Solomon Ossipovich Halperin, is engaged to Zachary Gavrilovich Mirkin, her father's assistant, whose grandfather and father have made a fortune in the timber business. The hero of the trilogy, Zachary, is a self-doubting introvert who falls under the spell of Halperin's wife, Olga Mihailovna, and has an affair with her. After contemplating suicide, he flees to Warsaw, while Nina marries his own father. The other two novels of the triptych chart his political and spiritual evolution towards a discovery of his hitherto suppressed Jewish identity and his involvement in the revolutionary struggle. The October Revolution, however, turns into a personal tragedy when his father is killed.

As the Asch scholar Mikhail Krutikov has shown in a recent essay, *Peterburg* is based on several historical figures. Halperin was probably inspired by Maksim Vinaver, the leader of the KD (Constitutional Democratic) party, who later held positions in the 1917 provisional government. Another character, the dance critic Boris Abramovich Levinstein, clearly stands for the famous critic Akim Volynskii (whose real name was Chaim Felkser), already featured in Asch's first novel, *Meri* (1912). Asch became acquainted with Volynskii, an early champion of Russian symbolism, through Khodotov.

Yet, for all the historical references (including one to the notorious Beilis affair, in which a Jew from Kiev was wrongly accused of murdering a Christian boy), Asch's picture of the Russian capital is a deeply symbolic one, contrasting the cosmopolitan, secular world of the Mirkins and Halperins with the brothel operated by Madame Kvasnetsova, who despite having converted to Christianity makes her establishment a refuge for illegal Jewish visitors to the city. One of them is Baruch Chomsky, leader of a Lithuanian community, who every evening curses the city in front of the Winter Palace, and indirectly initiates Zachary Mirkin's quest for his Jewish self. St. Petersburg is thus represented as a place of alienation. This powerful statement, as Krutikov has pointed out, is both a somewhat distorted picture of Jewish life in pre-revolutionary Petersburg, and a rather idealized one, including even an unexpectedly sympathetic view of Nicholas II.

Peterburg was published in Yiddish in 1929, followed by *Varshe* (*Warsaw*) the following year and *Moskve* (*Moscow*) in 1931. The three books appeared in English in 1933, in both London and New York, under the general title *Three cities, a trilogy*, in a translation (based on the German version) by the Scottish poet and literary scholar Edwin Muir and his wife Willa. That same year, Asch was unsuccessfully nominated for the Nobel Prize in Literature.

Asch and his wife lived in America from 1938 until 1953, when, partly owing to the campaign of hostility aroused by his Christological novels, they moved back to Europe, and finally to Israel. Asch died in London in 1957. The manuscript of *Peterburg* is part of the Sholem Asch papers acquired by Yale in 1944 through the generosity of Louis M. Rabinowitz.

Romanov Family Photographic Albums.

One of the most celebrated and prized photographic collections of the Beinecke Library, the six Romanov family photographic albums were originally in the possession of Anna Vyrubova, a close friend of Russia's last reigning family.

Great-granddaughter of Marshal Kutuzov, Anna Aleksandrovna Vyrubova was born in 1884, the daughter of the composer Aleksandr Sergeevich Taneev (1850–1918), who for many years was head of the Imperial Chancellery. She was appointed lady-in-waiting in 1903 but it was especially after 1906 that she gained the friendship of Tsarina Alexandra Feodorovna, of whom she became the chief confidante and preferred piano partner. In April 1907, Anna married Aleksei Vyrubov, a naval officer. This unhappy union was annulled a year later and she remained with the imperial family until 1917, despite a short crisis in early 1914, when it seems that the tsarina took umbrage at the affection Nicholas II was showing for her friend.

As Robert K. Massie has explained in his invaluable introduction to the selection from these albums published by the Vendome Press in 1982, most of the pictures, save for a few that are credited to the tsarina herself, were taken by court photographers who followed the imperial family. The photographs were pasted into albums by the tsarina and her family for their own records. Vyrubova, who evidently participated in those after-dinner sessions, had her own set of prints, and her own albums.

The professionalism of the anonymous photographers is evidenced by the remarkable quality of their work, especially in capturing intimate expressions on the faces of their imperial subjects. Indeed, apart from a few official occasions, such as military parades in front of the Catherine Palace at Tsarskoe Selo, the albums memorialize private moments in the lives of the last tsar's family: picnics, games of all seasons, sports, quiet reading or meditation, visits from friends and relatives. Even crowned heads of state, such as Edward VII and Queen Alexandra, royalty, like Prince George of Greece, or politicians, like Prime Minister Stolypin, are caught in unofficial, relaxed moods.

The six albums are traditionally numbered 2 to 7 (possibly after Vyrubova's own numbering). This numbering does not correspond to their chronology. The earliest photographs are to be found in Album 6, which covers the years 1907–09, followed by Album 5 (1908–09), Album 4 (1909–10), Album 7 (1910–11), Album 2 (1912–13), and Album 3 (chiefly 1912–15).

In addition to approximately 2400 photographs, the albums contain a few signed menus, printed concert programs, clippings, drawings, and caricatures. Some of the photographs are, in fact, postcards (such as the ones, in Album 3, showing the official declaration of war in August 1914). In some of the albums, especially in Album 5, some pictures were cut out, presumably by Vyrubova herself for presentation to friends; it can be noted that some of the photographs reproduced in her 1923 memoir are not to be found in the Beinecke albums. The existence or fate of a likely Album 1 is not clear, nor is the absence of any post-1915 photographs. Even though very few pictures in the albums were taken in St.

Petersburg proper, many show the life of the imperial family at their main residence, the Alexander Palace in Tsarskoe Selo, or when staying at other imperial palaces in the vicinity of Petersburg: Peterhof, Ropsha, Krasnoe Selo, and Pavlovsk in particular. Prince Iusupov, the future assassin of Rasputin, can be seen visiting Peterhof in 1909 in Album 5. Rasputin himself does not figure in the albums, even though he came on several occasions to Vyrubova's house in Tsarskoe Selo and she frequently acted as an emissary between him and the tsarina: she saw him for the last time at home a few hours before his death on 17/30 December 1916.

Many pictures were taken on the *Standart*, Nicholas's and Alexandra's favorite yacht, which took them on cruises in the Finnish fjords every June. Some document trips to the hunting lodge of Spala in Poland. Others show them in their favorite villegiatura on the coast of the Black Sea, Livadia, where a new palace—the future site of the Yalta conference—was erected in 1911. A special trip recorded in Album 7 is one undertaken in the fall of 1910 to Friedberg, in southern Germany, when it was decided that the tsarina's health might benefit from a visit to the neighboring spa of Bad Nauheim.

When the First World War broke out, the Catherine Palace at Tsarskoe Selo was converted into an infirmary. As can be seen from many 1915 pictures in Album 5, the empress, her daughters, and Anna all took training and served as nurses to wounded soldiers evacuated from the front. In early 1915, Vyrubova was nearly killed in a train crash when returning to St. Petersburg from Tsarskoe Selo.

The albums stop before the tragic events of 1917–18. After the tsar's abdication in March 1917, he and his family were detained at Tsarskoe Selo. Arrested shortly afterwards and interrogated several times, Vyrubova tried to flee through Finland but was rearrested and incarcerated for a while in the Peter and Paul Fortress. The correspondence between her and the empress and her daughters—also preserved in the Beinecke Library—ends in the summer of 1918 with a letter from Tobolsk, Siberia, shortly before the massacre of the entire family in Ekaterinburg on 18 July.

Vyrubova managed to escape from St. Petersburg to newly independent Finland in 1920. Her autobiography *Stranitsy iz moei zhizni*, published in 1923, was translated into English and came out in New York in the same year. Her diary for 1909–17, published in French, came out also in 1928, under the title *Le journal secret de Anna Viroubova*; in more recent times, it was published in Moscow in 1993. (The tsar and tsarina are referred to as Papa and Mama; as for Rasputin, he is simply the Starets.)

In 1937, Vyrubova received a visit from a Yale undergraduate from the class of 1939, Robert D. Brewster, a New Yorker who had befriended her brother, Sergei Taneev, after seeing the film *Rasputin and the empress*. The young man won Vyrubova's confidence and persuaded her to sell him the albums and her other Romanov memorabilia, which he in turn presented to his alma mater in 1951, with additional gifts in 1983. Vyrubova died in Helsinki in July 1964.

Tsarina Alexandra, in her nurse's uniform, is seen with her camera in the top picture; the group photograph below was taken by her.

Anastasia.

Feliks Iusupov at Peterhof.

The Alexander Palace at Tsarskoe Selo.

A salon in the Alexander Palace (showing Élisabeth Vigée-Lebrun's portrait of Marie-Antoinette and her children).

The Catherine Palace at Tsarskoe Selo, photographed by the tsarina.

Nikolai Ivanovich Berberov *and* Natalia Ivanovna Berberova. Autograph letters and postcards, signed, to Nina Berberova. Leningrad, 1927–43.

Nina Nikolaevna Berberova was born in St. Petersburg, in a house on Great Morskaia Street, on 26 July/8 August 1901. Russian on her mother's side, she was Armenian on her father's. Her paternal grandfather, Ivan Minaevich Berberian, was descended from Crimean Armenians who were protected by Catherine the Great and resettled by her on the Don near Rostov. The third of his seven sons, Nikolai Ivanovich, attended the Lazarevsky Institute of Oriental Languages in Moscow and was graduated in mathematics and physics from Moscow University. He joined the civil service, working in the ministry of finance, and by 1917 had reached the rank of state councillor.

Berberova joined Gumilev's Poets' Guild in 1921 and in 1922 published her first poem in the journal *Ushkuiniki*. That same year, she left Russia with the poet Vladislav Felitsianovich Khodasevich, whose life she shared until 1932. She returned only once, for a short visit to St. Petersburg and Moscow in the fall of 1989, four years after the French publication of her novella *The accompanist* made her one of the three most famous names of Russian émigré literature, along with Nabokov and Bunin. Like the former, Berberova emigrated to the United States. She taught in the Yale Slavic Department between 1958 and 1963 (having presented her archive to the Library the previous year), then at Princeton. In 1992, the year before she died, she received an honorary doctorate from Yale.

In her remarkable memoir, *Kursiv moi (The italics are mine)*, published first in an English translation by Philip Radley in 1969, and in Russian three years later, Berberova has left moving portraits of her parents and memories of growing up in St. Petersburg before the Revolution.

She also evokes her father's unexpected late career as a film actor, as a result of a chance meeting on Nevsky Prospect in 1935 with the Ukrainian director Grigorii Mikhailovich Kozintsev (1905–73), who needed a man of "his type" to play men of the "ancien régime" and gave him several such roles. In a memorable passage, she tells the story of joining a Communist cell in Paris in 1937, with the sole purpose of attending the screening of Kozintsev's *The Vyborg Side*, in which her father appeared. "The film was a story of a counterrevolutionary bastard, director of the State Bank, a saboteur and agent of a foreign power, who upset Lenin's restoration of the Russian budget. So Lenin sent a sailor from the Baltic fleet to the State Bank who, though he could neither read nor write, restored the financial balance of Russia in three days. (The affair took place in 1918.) The director of the bank was arrested together with his cronies, and on the screen and in the hall the crowd screamed wildly, 'Beat him! Hit him in the teeth! Chop down the enemies of the working class!' At the last moment my father managed to pour ink onto the open page of a ledger, proving that he would oppose Lenin's deed to his last breath. They led him to the exit. At the gates of the State Bank, he was given a minute to stop, look at the Ekaterinsky Canal, at the Petersburg sky, growing turbid with rain, and straight at me, sitting in the Paris hall. Our eyes met. He was led away under escort. I never saw him again. But several words that he uttered brought back his voice, his smile, his quick hazel-eyed glance that spoke without words. After fifteen years of separation, what a meeting! The joy of meeting after such a separation and before parting forever is not preordained for everyone."

Immediately after this passage, Berberova briefly reconstitutes in her imagination the fate of her parents during the siege in the winter of 1941–42, after which they were evacuated. Her mother died en route, her father some time later, in an unknown place.

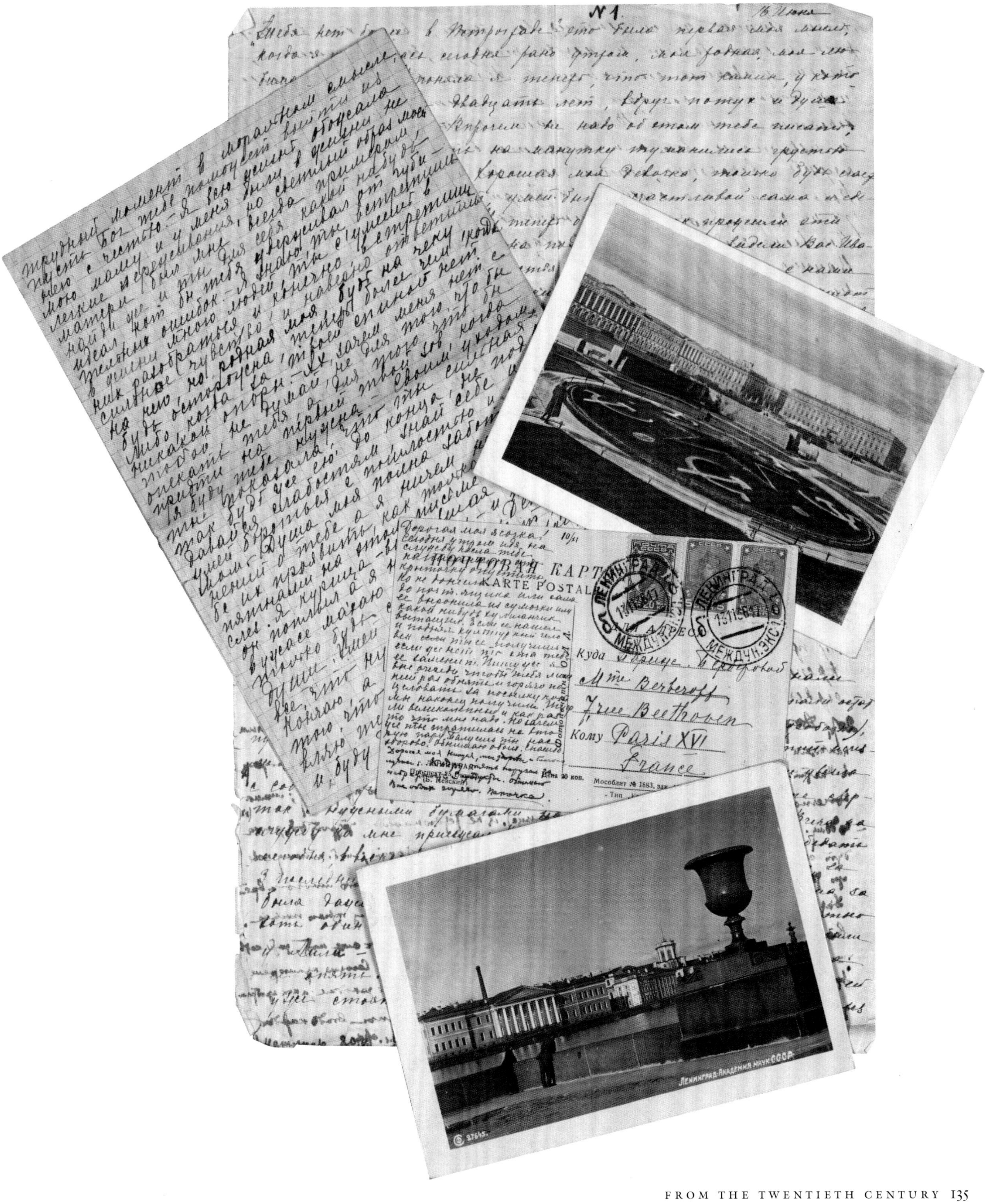

N 1.

Mme Berberoff
7 rue Beethoven
Paris XVI
France

Anna Akhmatova. *Poema bez geroia: triptich, 1940–1955.* Leningrad, Tashkent, Moscow, 1955. Typescript with holograph corrections.

One of the two great Russian women poets of the twentieth century and one of the great Petersburg poets, Akhmatova, whose original name was Anna Andreevna Gorenko, was born in Crimea on 11 June 1889. She grew up in Tsarskoe Selo and was educated both in Kiev and St. Petersburg. She made her literary debut as a member of the Acmeist group, an off-shoot of the symbolist movement. Between 1910 and 1918 she was married to one of the leaders of the group, the poet Niko-lai Gumilev, who was shot by the Bolsheviks in 1921. Her first collection, *Vecher* (Evening), came out in 1912 under the pseudonym Anna Akhmatova, which was the name of her Tatar great-grandmother. It was followed by *Chetki* (Rosary) in 1914 and *U samogo moria* (By the very sea) in 1915. Although she decided to remain in Russia after the Revolution, she was treated as an "internal émigrée" and, except for a brief period in 1940–43, was not allowed to publish between *Anno domini MCMXXI*, issued in Petersburg in 1922, and 1958. Expelled from the Union of Soviet Writers in 1946, she supported herself chiefly with translation work. For nearly three decades, from 1926 to 1952, save for three years in Tashkent during the Second World War, she lived in an apartment in a wing of the former Sheremetev Palace (then called Fontannyi Dom, Fountain House) on the Fontanka, where she had settled briefly in 1918 with Gumilev; it has now become the Anna Akhmatova Museum. She died in Domodedovo, near Moscow, on 5 March 1966.

Along with *Requiem* (1935–40), her long poem devoted to the memory of the victims of Stalin's terror, which was published only in 1963, *Poem without a hero* is considered one of her masterpieces. She worked on it from 1940 on, revising it until her death. Part of it appeared in 1958 in the verse collection *Beg vremini* (The course of time), but typescripts, such as the one in the Beinecke's collections, were circulated, reflecting earlier versions (the final title is dated 1940–1962). In the Beinecke typescript, Akhmatova added the non-cyrillic words and phrases and various decorations in her own hand, as well as her signature on the last page.

The poem takes as its epigraph the motto of the Shereme-tev family, "Deus conservat omnia" and is preceded by a double foreword, dated Tashkent, 8 April 1943 and Leningrad, November 1944. Then follow two dedications, the first to the memory of the young poet Vsevolod Kniazev, whose bien-aimée was involved with the symbolist poet Aleksandr Blok, the second (here spelled out, whereas the final printed version bears only the initials) to Akhmatova's friend the actress Olga Afanasevna Glebova-Sudeikina, who died in Paris in 1945. (A third dedication, anonymous but in fact to Isaiah Berlin, who visited Akhmatova in 1945 and 1946, was added in 1956.)

The first part of the poem, "The year 1913: a Petersburg tale," headed here by a single Byron epigraph (two more were added), was inspired by the suicide of Kniazev. It comprises three chapters. In the first are found the vision of a masquerade, an apostrophe to Glebova-Sudeikina, a reminiscence of Tsarskoe Selo combined and a ghostlike vision of the Champ-de-Mars, where a formal ball coincides with the poet's last moments; the Tsarskoe Selo and Champ-de-Mars parts form two separate sections in the published version. The second part, "Tails" (or "The other side of the coin"), subtitled "Intermezzo," is dated "3–5 January 1942, Fountain House," where it is set, supposedly in January 1941. Beginning as a dialogue with a dissatisfied editor, it is a reflection by the poet on her work. It comprises seventeen verses instead of the twenty-four of the final version, in which two stanzas (not present here) are made of lines of dots (a clear reference to censorship) and one is presented as incomplete. The third part, "Epilogue," begins with the famous line from Pushkin's *Bronze Horseman* ("I love you, Peter's own creation . . .") and a dedication "To my city." It takes place on the White Night of 24 June 1942, while the author, then evacuated to Tashkent, meditates on the destroyed, besieged city and its dead. This last part is dated Tashkent, 18 August 1942.

ПОЭМА БЕЗ ГЕРОЯ

триптих

1940 - 1955

сочинение

АННЫ АХМАТОВОЙ

Ленинград - Ташкент - Москва

1955

Не дождался желанных вестниц...

Над тобой - лишь твоих прелестниц,

Белых ноченек, хоровод.

А веселое слово - дома -

Никому теперь не знакомо,

Все в чужое глядят окно.

Кто в Ташкенте, кто в Нью-Иорке,

И изгнания воздух горький -

Как отравленное вино.

Все вы мной любоваться могли бы,

Когда в брюхе летучей рыбы

Я от злой погони спаслась

И над Ладогой и над лесом,]

Словно   т а,   одержимая бесом,

Как на Брокен ночной неслась...

И уже предо мною прямо

Леденела и стыла Кама,

И *quo vadis?* 1X/ кто то сказал,

Но не дал шевельнуть устами,

Как тоннелями и мостами

Загремел сумасшедший Урал.

От того, что сделалось прахом,

Обуянная смертным страхом

И отмщения зная срок,

Опустивши глаза сухие

И ломая руки, Россия

Предо мною шла на восток.

А. Ахматова.

Окончено в Ташкенте
18 августа 1942 года.

Selected Bibliography

Akhmatova, Anna. *The complete poems*. Translated by Judith Hemschemeyer; edited with an introduction by Roberta Reeder. Somerville, Mass.: Zephyr Press, 1990.

Asch, Sholem. *Three cities*. New York: Carroll and Graf, 1983.

Bely, Andrey. *Petersburg*. Translated, annotated, and introduced by Robert A. Maguire and John E. Malmstad. Bloomington: Indiana University Press, 1978.

Berberova, Nina. *The italics are mine*. Translated by Philip Radley. New York: Vintage Books, 1993. (First edition 1969)

Berelowitch, Wladimir, and Olga Medvedkova. *Histoire de Saint-Pétersbourg*. Paris: Fayard, 1996.

Bouatchidzé, Gaston. *La vie de Marie Brosset*. Nantes: Éditions du Petit Véhicule [1996].

Bushkovitch, Paul. *Peter the Great: the struggle for power, 1671–1725*. Cambridge & New York: Cambridge University Press, 2001.

Cadot, Michel. *La Russie dans la vie intellectuelle française, 1839–1856*. Paris: Fayard, 1967.

Clark, Katerina. *Petersburg, Crucible of Cultural Revolution*. Cambridge: Harvard University Press, 1995

Custine, Astolphe marquis de. *La Russie en 1839*. Paris: Solin, 1990.

Dumas, Alexandre. *En Russie: impressions de voyage*. Paris: F. Bourin, 1989.

Dvoichenko-Markoff, Eufrosina. "Benjamin Franklin, the American Philosophical Society, and the Russian Academy of Sciences." In *Proceedings of the American Philosophical Society* XCI (1947), p. 251.

Gautier, Théophile. *Voyage en Russie*. Présentation du texte et des notes par Francine-Dominique Liechtenham. Paris: La boîte à documents, 1990.

Krutikov, Mikhail. "Russia between Myth and Reality. From *Meri* to *Three Cities*." In *Sholem Asch reconsidered*, edited by Nanette Stahl. New Haven: Beinecke Rare Book and Manuscript Library, Yale University, 2003. See also, in the same volume, Wolitz, Seth L. "The City as Cadre and Character in Sholem Asch's *Dray Shtet*."

Maistre, Joseph de. *Les soirées de Saint-Pétersbourg, ou, Entretiens sur le gouvernement temporel de la Providence*. Édition critique sous la direction de Jean-Louis Darcel. Geneva: Slatkine, 1993.

Maistre, Joseph de. *St. Petersburg Dialogues, or, Conversations on the temporal government of Providence*. Translated and edited by Richard A. Lebrun. Montreal & Kingston: McGill-Queen's University Press, 1993.

[Makhaev, Mikhail Ivanovich.] *Vidy Peterburga i ego okrestnostei serediny XVIII veka. Graviury po rysunkam M. Makhaeva*. Leningrad: Sov. khudozhnik, 1968.

Massie, Robert K., and Marilyn Pfeifer Swezey. *The Romanov Family Album*. New York and Paris: The Vendome Press, 1982.

Meaux, Lorraine de, ed. *Saint-Pétersbourg: histoire, promenades, anthologie et dictionnaire*. Paris: Robert Laffont, 2003 (Collection Bouquins).

Muhlstein, Anka. *A taste for freedom: the life of Astolphe de Custine*. Translated by Teresa Waugh. New York: Helen Marx Books, 1999.

Phillips, Catherine, and Christopher and Melanie Rice [et al.] *St. Petersburg*. London, New York etc.: Dorling Kindersley Publishing, Inc., 1998, revised ed. 2001. (DK Eyewitness Travel Guides)

Phillips-Matz, Mary-Jane. *Verdi: a biography*. With a foreword by Andrew Porter. Oxford & New York: Oxford University Press, 1993.

Pushkin, Aleksandr Sergeevich. *The Bronze Horseman*, in *The poems, prose and plays of Alexander Pushkin*, selected and edited, with an introduction by Avrahm Yarmolinsky. New York: The Modern Library, 1936.

Réau, Louis. *Saint-Pétersbourg*. Paris: H. Laurens, 1913.

Sadie, Stanley, editor. *The New Grove Dictionary of Music and Musicians*. London: Macmillan; New York: Grove's Dictionaries, 2001. Entries Cimarosa, Galuppi, Manfredini, Paisiello, Sarti, Traetta.

[Sadovnikov, Vasilii Semenovich.] *Vasilii Semenovich Sadovnikov 1800–1879*. [Exhibition catalogue.] St. Petersburg: Gosudarstvennii Russkii Muzei; Palace Editions, 2000.

Schakovskoy, Zinaida, Princess. *La vie quotidienne à Saint-Pétersbourg à l'époque romantique*. Paris: Hachette, 1967.

Schenker, Alexander M. *The Bronze Horseman*. New Haven: Yale University Press, 2003.

Tarn, Julien-Frédéric. *Le marquis de Custine, ou, Les malheurs de l'exactitude*. Paris: Fayard, 1985.

Vyrubova, Anna Aleksandrovna. *Memories of the Russian Court*. New York: Macmillan, 1923.

Index of Names

Index of Places
and institutions in and around St. Petersburg

EDITORIAL STYLING
James Mooney

DESIGN
Greer Allen

TYPESETTING
Bessas & Ackerman

COLOR SEPARATION
Professional Graphics, Inc.

PRINTING
Thames Printing Company

BINDING
Acme Bookbinding Company